The Wit, Wisdom and

Baseball's

Wisecracks of

Greatest

America's National

Quotes

Pastime

Compiled by

Kevin Nelson

A Fireside Book
Published by Simon and Schuster
New York

For My Father

All rights reserved
including the right of reproduction
in whole or in part in any form
A Fireside Book
Published by Simon & Schuster, Inc.
Simon & Schuster Building
Rockefeller Center
1230 Avenue of the Americas
New York, New York 10020
FIRESIDE and colophon are registered trademarks of
Simon & Schuster, Inc.
Designed by Irving Perkins Associates
Manufactured in the United States of America
Printed and bound by The Murray Printing Co.
7 8 9 10

Library of Congress Cataloging in Publication Data
Main entry under title:
Baseball's greatest quotes.
"A Fireside book."
Includes index.
1. Baseball—United States—Quotations, maxims,
etc.   I. Nelson, Kevin, date.
GV867.3.B37   796.357′0207   81-21352
AACR2
ISBN 0-671-43474-8

Contents

Preface

○ BASEBALL IS the most quotable of games. Its literature and oral traditions are so rich and wonderfully vast that it's hard to think of any other sport which compares to it. Only baseball, after all, has produced such a preeminent philosopher as Casey Stengel—and you can look it up.

In baseball, unlike sports ruled by the clock, there is always plenty of time. Perhaps that's why so many fine writers like the game. Maybe that's also why so many screwballs are drawn to it. On the lazy, sun-drenched afternoons of baseball, there is always time to tell a good story or swap jokes. Out of this easy, youthful banter come the one-liners and wisecracks—the gentle breezes of inspiration, if you will—that largely make up this book.

Bernard Malamud has said that "the whole history of baseball has the quality of mythology," and certainly this is true when it comes to the telling of stories. Many great lines and anecdotes have been told and retold for so long that they are practically without origin. Stan Musial, undaunted by the prospect of facing Dodger spitballer Preacher Roe, says he'll just stand up there and hit the dry side of Roe's spitter; some twenty-five years later, Bobby Murcer remarks that he'll handle Gaylord Perry by hitting the dry side of *his* spitter.

While this perpetually circulating river of lore is one of baseball's most appealing traits, trying to determine who said what when can be like Abbott and Costello trying to figure out who's on first. You could feed an entire Little League team with all the lamb chops that great hurlers supposedly could throw past wolves. Similarly, there must be dozens of Yogi Berra yarns—some of them even true—all with their own variations. My purpose here is not to set the record straight but simply to present it.

7

A few words must be said about the book's organization. Because wit is probably best appreciated within its own time, the selections in chapters two through ten are arranged, for the most part, chronologically. If the date of a remark is unknown, it's placed by the player's or manager's career. If someone performed in more than one era, his remarks may appear in a couple of chapters. Some exemplary players and teams, like Ted Williams or the 1975 Cincinnati Reds, have transcended time, and their stories are told all at once.

It should be added that the historical divisions are meant to be regarded only as guideposts. If they encourage debate 'round the old hot stove, so much the better. *The Baseball Encyclopedia*, published by Macmillan, was my primary source of statistical information and shall have the last say in all disputes.

Many more people than I could possibly thank have played no small part in the making of this book. Duffy Jennings and the entire San Francisco Giants' organization, William Ramirez at the San Francisco Public Library, and Wes Mathis at the National Library of Sports in San Jose freely made their facilities available to me. Charles Einstein, Clifford Kachline, Historian at the National Baseball Hall of Fame in Cooperstown, and Gary Cohen of Major League Baseball Promotions were generous with their time and expertise. Nat Andriani of United Press International was an invaluable aid in photo research. Thanks must also go to my agent, Amy Rennert, who helped start me on this project. Most especially, I owe a great debt to Ruthe Stein, whose encouragement, advice and typewriter were a blessing throughout.

—KEVIN NELSON

Acknowledgments

GRATEFUL ACKNOWLEDGMENT is made to the following for permission to reprint selections included in this book:

Thomas Albright.

Associated Features, Inc., for *The Wit and Wisdom of Yogi Berra* by Phil Pepe, copyright © 1974 by Associated Features, Inc.

Doubleday & Company, Inc., for *Charlie O. & the Angry A's* by Bill Libby, copyright © 1975 by Mattgo Enterprises, Inc., reprinted by permission of Doubleday & Company, Inc.; *My Life in Baseball* by Ty Cobb with Al Stump, copyright © 1961 by Doubleday and Company, Inc., reprinted by permission of the publisher.

Farrar, Straus and Giroux, Inc., for an excerpt from "My Baseball Years" from *Reading Myself and Others* by Philip Roth. Copyright © 1973,1975 by Philip Roth, reprinted by permission of Farrar, Straus and Giroux, Inc.

Harper & Row, Publishers, Inc., for specified 5 quotations from *You Can't Beat the Hours* by Mel Allen and Ed Fitzgerald, copyright © 1964 by Mel Allen and Ed Fitzgerald, reprinted by permission of Harper & Row, Publishers, Inc.; specified excerpts from *The Boys of Summer* by Roger Kahn, copyright © 1971, 1972 by Roger Kahn, reprinted by permission of Harper & Row, Publishers, Inc.

Houghton Mifflin Company. From *The Ultimate Baseball Book* edited by Daniel Okrent and Harris Lewine. Copyright © 1979, 1981 by The Hilltown Press, Inc. and Harris Lewine. Reprinted by permission of Houghton Mifflin Company.

Alfred A. Knopf, Inc., for specified excerpts from *Assorted Prose*, by John Updike. Copyright © 1960 by John Updike. Reprinted by permission of Alfred A. Knopf, Inc. Originally appeared in *The New Yorker*.

Little, Brown and Company, for two excerpts from *God's Country And Mine* by Jacques Barzun, copyright © 1954 by Jacques Barzun, reprinted by permission of Little, Brown and Company in association with the Atlantic Monthly Press.

Macmillan Publishing Co., Inc., from *The Glory Of Their Times,* by Lawrence S. Ritter, copyright © 1966 by Lawrence S. Ritter, reprinted by permission of Macmillan Publishing Co.; for *The American Sporting Scene* by John Kieran. Ills. by Joseph W. Golinkin (copyright © 1941 by John

9

Introduction

O I SAT on the Polo Grounds bench alone that soggy summer afternoon in 1962. The Mets were three months old and I was twenty-nine years old. In baseball talk we were all rookies.

This gnarled old man soon appeared from a runway. He hopped as he walked from an old foot injury when a taxicab nailed him in Boston. You could look it up here in Kevin Nelson's splendid collection of words and music—all baseball talk is music to the true devotee's ears—and find out what one sportswriter had to say about that.

Casey Stengel was at my side. Stengelese rushed from his mouth the way water falls from the Niagara. He was in full voice that day, his head moving from side to side, his hands slapping his chest and mine, his eyes wide and alert, his voice cracking through the stillness of a languid day. A television broadcaster soon appeared.

"How about an interview?" he asked.

"Don't you see I'm talking to my writers," Stengel announced.

When I searched the bench and saw I was still alone with this master elocutionist, I realized I had been nominated for baseball writing sainthood. I was one of Casey's "writers," those cherished few among us he would reward with word and wisdom because we had proven loyal to the game of baseball.

There are only so many line drive doubles and grand slam home runs and two-hit shutouts any of us can witness.

We are all linked, we baseball junkies, by the printed word. The messengers who have helped us span the ages of baseball are Franklin P. Adams and Red Smith and Grantland Rice and Westbrook Pegler and Ernest Hemingway, whose Old Man loved the great DiMaggio so. And Stengel and McGraw and Billy Martin and Frankie Frisch.

11

Had a man ever expressed truer love for another than Johnny Keane when he said of Bob Gibson, "I have a commitment to his heart"? Has the agony of defeat ever been better categorized than when these words came from the hangdog being of a manager named Wes Westrum after another in the series of endless Mets losses: "Oh, my God, wasn't that awful?"

For more than a hundred years, through global wars and international depressions, through player raids and player strikes, through agony and ecstasy, baseball has been captured by the printed word. The writers and the managers and the players passed their vivid recollections of the game, of America and of ourselves on through the century.

Now in one brilliant stroke Kevin Nelson has put some of the best things ever said about the game, and about all of us, under one roof. This collection tells the story of baseball through the eyes of those who were there: Muggsy McGraw, who would harpoon a writer with his piercing eyes for calling him that in print; Casey Stengel, who retired to a Glendale bank and placed a sign saying "Stengelese Spoken Here" on his bare desk to announce that he was open for business; and Joe McCarthy, who admitted he didn't know if DiMaggio could bunt but announced, "I'll never find out, either."

So much of our history is communicated within these pages. It is not just baseball that is recorded here but America, a sweeter America, an easier America, a more joyous America.

We have leaned on language to make us one. From Maine to Mississippi, from Minnesota to Montana, from New York to New Mexico, we struggle to speak the same language, our ears laboring to catch the nuances of different geography. There are no nuances in baseball; there are only bunts and bingles, flakes and phonies, grand slams and hot dogs. To love baseball is to love the language of the game.

We thank Kevin Nelson for *Baseball's Greatest Quotes*. We slide downriver gracefully now into a sea of comment on the game, a journey as joyous as any Mark Twain ever took talkin' down the Mississippi.

—MAURY ALLEN

1
OUR
NATIONAL
PASTIME

○ BASEBALL IS America's game. Since around the middle of the last century we've been happily playing it and watching it. Kids, poets, presidents, thieves, senators, generals, shop clerks, steelworkers, movie stars, teamsters, farmers, writers, all have been drawn to the game and been moved by it. Baseball is in our language, our history, our blood. Without it, as the novelist James T. Farrell has suggested, the world would be far different for many of us.

Whoever wants to know the heart and mind of America had better learn baseball.

—JACQUES BARZUN

Baseball has stood for loyalty to the verities, memories of innocence, patience with ritual; surely no one who cared about baseball could be an opportunist at heart.

—EDWARD HOAGLAND

13

Franklin D. Roosevelt throws out the first ball of the Washington Senators' 1935 season, while two future Hall-of-Famers—Clark Griffith and Bucky Harris—and twenty thousand fans look on. "At the baseball match, we encounter real democracy of spirit. . . . Barriers are forgotten and how good it seems for us to be just human beings"—Reverend Roland D. Sawyer.

I see great things in baseball. It's our game—the American game. It will take our people out-of-doors, fill them with oxygen, give them a larger physical stoicism. Tend to relieve us from being a nervous, dyspeptic set. Repair these losses, and be a blessing to us.

—WALT WHITMAN

Baseball has been one of the greatest pleasures of my life. I have seen 906 speaking plays, 1,050 movies, and I have attended 4,510 church services and read 2,000 books; but I think I have gotten most good out of my 1,134 ball games.

—FREDERICK S. TYLER

It is the best of all games for me. It frequently escapes from ae pattern of sport and assumes the form of a virile ballet. It is purer than any dance because the actions of the players are not governed by music or crowded into a formula by a director. The movement is natural and unrehearsed and controlled only by the unexpected flight of the ball.

—JIMMY CANNON

Most people go out to the ballpark to watch the home team win. I go to see a unique spectacle of avant-garde art: performance, conceptualism, surrealist ritual, psychodrama, dance—where else can you find a more perfect union of all these forms than in a game of baseball?

—THOMAS ALBRIGHT, art critic

The scene is instant, whole and wonderful. In its beauty and design that vision of the soaring stands, the pattern of forty thousand empetalled faces, the velvet and unalterable geometry of the playing field, and the small lean figures of the players, set there, lonely, tense and waiting in their places, bright, desperate solitary atoms encircled by that huge wall of nameless faces, is incredible.

—THOMAS WOLFE, *Of Time and the River*

For someone whose roots in America were strong but only inches deep, and who had no experience, such as a Catholic child might, of an awesome hierarchy that was real and felt, baseball was a kind of secular church that reached into every class and region of the nation and bound millions upon millions of us together in common concerns, loyalties, rituals, enthusiasms, and antagonisms. Baseball made me understand what patriotism was about, at its best.

—PHILIP ROTH

15

Baseball has done more to move America in the right direction than all the professional patriots with their billions of cheap words.

—MONTE IRVIN

There is something uniquely American in hitting one out of the park.

—DICK YOUNG

Whenever a player hits the ball out of the park I have a sense of elation. I feel as if I had done it. To me, every wall or fence is palpably an inhibition. Beyond the bleacher roof lies Italy. . . .

—HEYWOOD BROUN

The fundamental reason for the popularity of the game is the fact that it is a national safety valve. . . . That is what baseball does for humanity. It serves the same purpose as a revolution in Central America or a thunderstorm on a hot day. . . . So long as it remains our national game, America will abide no monarchy, and anarchy will be too slow.

—ALLEN SANGREE (1907)

Baseball is the American success story. . . . It is, moreover, a great common ground on which bartenders and bishops, clergymen and bosses, bankers and laborers meet with true equality and understanding. The game has proved in everyday language that democracy works.

—J. G. TAYLOR SPINK

Baseball is very big with my people. It figures. It's the only time we can get to shake a bat at a white man without starting a riot.

—DICK GREGORY

There were things about the games I liked. The crowds, for example. I felt like I was part of something there, you know, like in church, except it was more real than any church, and I joined in the scorekeeping, hollering, the eating of hot dogs and drinking of Cokes and beer, and for a while I even had the idea that ball stadiums, and not European churches were the real American holy places.

—ROBERT COOVER

Vida Blue. "There is excitement in the game, but little beauty except in the long-limbed 'pitcher'. . . . In his efforts to combine speed, mystery, and curve, he gets into attitudes of a very novel and fantastic, but quite obvious beauty"—Rupert Brooke.

The little red school house has long been extolled as a prime factor in the republic's progress. I for one am firmly convinced that the lessons taught in it would have lacked much of their potency had it not been for the reinforcement they received from the lessons learned on the baseball field nearby. Long may Uncle Sam play ball!

—H. ADDINGTON BRUCE (1913)

By and large it is the sport that a foreigner is least likely to take to. You have to grow up playing it, you have to accept the lore of the bubble-gum card, and believe that if the answer to the Mays-Snider-Mantle question is found, then the universe will be a simpler and more ordered place.

—DAVID HALBERSTAM

Baseball has the great advantage over cricket of being ended sooner. . . . It combines the best features of that primitive form of cricket known as Tip and Run with those of lawn tennis, Puss-in-the-corner and Handel's Messiah.

—GEORGE BERNARD SHAW

Knowin' all about baseball is just about as profitable as bein' a good whittler.

—ABE MARTIN, humorist

With those who don't give a damn about baseball, I can only sympathize. I do not resent them. I am even willing to concede that many of them are physically clean, good to their mothers and in favor of world peace. But while the game is on, I can't think of anything to say to them.

—ART HILL, author

One reason I have always loved baseball so much is that it has been not merely "the great national game," but really a part of the whole weather of our lives, of the thing that is our own, of the whole fabric, the million memories of America. For example, in the memory of almost every one of us, is there anything that can evoke spring—the first fine days of April—better than the sound of the ball smacking into the pocket of the big mitt, the sound of the bat as it hits the horsehide; for me . . . almost everything I know about spring is in it—the first leaf, the jonquil, the maple tree, the smell of grass upon your hands and knees, the coming into flower of April.

—THOMAS WOLFE (1938)

That's the true harbinger of spring, not crocuses or swallows returning to Capistrano, but the sound of a bat on a ball.

—BILL VEECK, former baseball owner

It breaks your heart. It is designed to break your heart. The game begins in the spring, when everything else begins again, and it blossoms in the summer, filling the afternoons and evenings, and then as soon as the chill rains come, it stops and leaves you to face the fall alone.

—A. BARTLETT GIAMATTI

Baseball is continuous, like nothing else among American things, an endless game of repeated summers, joining the long generations of all the fathers and all the sons.

—DONALD HALL, poet

And I suspect that I was not singular in the way in which I looked upon baseball and dreamed of it [*as a child*]. *It was no mere game. It was an extension of my inner feelings and hopes. My favorite players were like my ambassadors to the world. They were doing what I was too small to do.*

—JAMES T. FARRELL

Billy Martin and Terry Cooney. "It is wonderful to be here, to be able to hear the baseball against the bat, ball against glove, and be able to boo the umpire"
—General Douglas MacArthur.

New York celebrates the Mets' 1969 World Series win. "Great is baseball, the national tonic, the reviver of hope, the restorer of confidence"—*Baseball Magazine*.

When I was a boy growing up in Kansas, a friend of mine and I went fishing and as we sat there in the warmth of a summer afternoon on a river bank we talked about what we wanted to do when we grew up. I told him I wanted to be a real major league baseball player, a genuine professional like Honus Wagner. My friend said that he'd like to be President of the United States. Neither of us got our wish.

—DWIGHT DAVID EISENHOWER

I've had a lifelong ambition to be a professional baseball player, but nobody would sign me.

—GERALD FORD

Thank God for center field! Doctor, you can't imagine how truly glorious it is out there, so alone in all that space. . . . Do you know baseball at all? Because center field is like some observation post, a kind of control tower, where you are able to see everything and everyone, to understand what's happening the instant it happens, not only by the sound of the struck bat, but by the spark of movement that goes through the infielders in the first second that the ball comes flying at them; and once it gets beyond them, "It's mine," you call, "it's mine," and then after it you go. For in center field, if you can get it, it is yours. Oh, how unlike my home it is to be in center field, where no one will appropriate unto himself anything that I say is mine!

—PHILIP ROTH, *Portnoy's Complaint*

No game in the world is as tidy and dramatically neat as baseball, with cause and effect, crime and punishment, motive and result, so cleanly defined.

—PAUL GALLICO

Baseball is a serious thing in this country, and if that reveals our immaturity, I suppose there is little we can do about it until we grow up.

—LARAINE DAY

Wars are declared, fought and ended. Elections are called, held and decided. Floods rise, ravage and subside. And each has its transient hold upon the populace. But to the American in whose veins the wine of April is bubbling there is nothing which has the perennial fascination [of] baseball.

—NEW YORK EVENING *Sun* (1915)

I believe that all men who have ever lived and achieved success in this world had lived in vain if they knew not baseball.

—SENATOR CHAUNCEY DEPEW

21

2
FROM CRADLE TO SHAME: 1876–1920

○ THOSE YOUNG fans accustomed to the polished veneer of baseball today may be surprised to learn that it hasn't always been that way. In the late 1800s baseball was a rowdy and thoroughly incorrigible game, the kind of thing Huck Finn might have liked if he were inclined to sports. That baseball grew up to be a profession loved and respected by millions is largely due to men like Connie Mack, John McGraw, Ty Cobb and Christy Mathewson. Their wondrous skills and inspired play transformed the game and made it, in all important respects, a mirror of the one we see now.

EARLY VOICES

Baseball is the very symbol, the outward and visible expression of the drive and push and rush and struggle of the raging, tearing, booming nineteenth century.

—MARK TWAIN

I would rather be president of the Cincinnati baseball club than President of the United States.

> —AARON B. CHAMPION, president of the
> Cincinnati baseball club, the Red Stockings
> (1869)

Baseball was mighty and exciting to me, but there is no blinking at the fact that at the time the game was thought, by solid sensible people, to be only one degree above grand larceny, arson and mayhem.

> —CONNIE MACK (circa 1888)

PLEASE DO NOT SHOOT THE UMPIRE;
HE IS DOING THE BEST HE CAN.

> —Sign at Kansas City ball park (1882)

Mother, may I slug the umpire,
May I slug him right away?
So he cannot be here, mother,
When the clubs begin to play?
Let me clasp his throat, dear mother,
In a dear, delightful grip,
With one hand and with the other
Bat him several in the lip.
Let me climb his frame, dear mother,
While the happy people shout,
I'll not kill him, dearest mother,
I will only knock him out.
Let me mop the ground up, mother,
With his person, dearest, do,
If the ground can stand it, mother,
I don't see why you can't, too.

> —Anonymous fan (1886)

This is a funny business. We get paid to knock the cover off the ball, and pitchers get paid to keep us from hitting it.

> —BUG HOLLIDAY, Reds outfielder

Yeah? What league was he in?

> —PETE BROWNING, outfielder, on hearing of
> the assassination of President James Garfield
> in 1881

The good time is approaching,
  The season is at hand.
When the merry click of the two-base lick
  Will be heard throughout the land.
The frost still lingers on the earth, and
  Budless are the trees.
But the merry ring of the voice of spring
  Is borne upon the breeze.

> —Ode to Opening Day, *The Sporting News*
> (1886)

The Americans have a genius for taking a thing, examining its every part, and developing each part to the utmost. This they have done with the [English] game of rounders, and, from a clumsy, primitive pastime, have so tightened its joints and put such a fine finish on its points that it stands forth a complicated machine of infinite exactitude.

> —ANGUS EVAN ABBOTT, English commentator,
> on baseball in the early 1900s

JOHN McGRAW'S GIANTS

It's great to be young and a New York Giant.

> —LARRY DOYLE, Giants second baseman (circa
> 1914)

It has always been my ambition to play in New York City. Brooklyn is all right, but if you're not with the Giants, you might as well be in Albany.

> —BILL DAHLEN, Giants shortstop

They's a flock of pitchers that knows a batter's weakness and works accordin'. But they ain't nobody else in the world that can stick a ball as near where they want to stick it as he can. . . . I ain't tryin' to make you believe that he don't never fail to pitch where he's aimin' at. If he done that, he wouldn't be here; he'd be workin' agin the angels in St. Peter's League. But he's got ten to one better control than any guy I ever seen, and I've saw the best o' them.

> —RING LARDNER, on Christy Mathewson

24

Mathewson pitched against Cincinnati yesterday. Another way of putting it is that Cincinnati lost a game of baseball. The first statement means the same as the second.

> —DAMON RUNYON

It is in the pinch that the pitcher shows whether or not he is a Big Leaguer. . . . He needs a head, and he has to use it. It is the acid test. That is the reason so many men, who shine in the minor leagues, fail to make good in the majors. They cannot stand the fire.

> —CHRISTY MATHEWSON (1912)

In addition to physical ability, Mathewson had the perfect temperament for a ballplayer. Always he sought to learn something new, and he never forgot what he had learned in the past. He had everything—strength, intelligence, courage and willingness.

> —BOZEMAN BULGER, *New York Evening World* (1923)

A pitcher's speed is worth nothing if he cannot put the ball where he wants to. To me, control is the first requirement of good pitching.

> —CHRISTY MATHEWSON

His game of life was called by the darkness of death, but the Great Manager of all, releasing from mortal pain and travail, has taken him home, and signed him to an eternity of light and happiness.

> —MAYOR JAMES CURLEY of Boston, eulogizing Mathewson at his death in 1925. Grantland Rice, another fan of Matty's, called him "the knightliest of all the game's paladins."

Matty was master of them all.

> —Last line of Mathewson's plaque in the Hall of Fame

Bugs drank a lot, you know, and sometimes it seemed like the more he drank the better he pitched. They used to say he didn't spit on the ball: he blew his breath on it, and the ball would come up drunk.

> —RUBE MARQUARD, reminiscing about Giants teammate Bugs Raymond

There has been only one manager, and his name is John McGraw.

—CONNIE MACK

He'd walk up and down the dugout and yell, "Wipe those damned smiles off your face." He'd warn players against becoming buddy-buddy with sportswriters. One rookie was really scared. When a writer asked, "Are you married?" the rookie answered, "You'd better ask Mr. McGraw."

—ROGERS HORNSBY

With my team I am an absolute czar.

—JOHN MCGRAW

Do you know what the cardinal sin was on that ball club? To begin a sentence to McGraw with the words "I thought . . ." "You thought?" he would yell. "With what?"

—FRED LINDSTROM, Giants third baseman

In playing or managing, the game of ball is only fun for me when I'm out in front and winning. I don't care a bag of peanuts for the rest of the game.

—JOHN MCGRAW

I have seen McGraw go on to ball fields where he is as welcome as a man with the black smallpox. . . . I have seen him take all sorts of personal chances. He doesn't know what fear is.

—CHRISTY MATHEWSON

McGraw's very walk across the field in a hostile town was a challenge to the multitude.

—GRANTLAND RICE

I suppose it was an important part of McGraw's great capacity for leadership that he would take kids out of the coal mines and out of the wheat fields and make them walk and talk and chatter and play ball with the look of eagles.

—HEYWOOD BROUN

26

John McGraw, iron-willed manager of the New York Giants. One time a player, ignoring orders to bunt, swung away and hit a home run—and was slapped with a fine. Said McGraw, "I permit no deviations from instructions."

My years in baseball had their ups and downs, their strife and their torment. But the years I look back at most fondly, and those I'd like most to live over, are the years when I was playing center field for the New York Giants.

—FRED SNODGRASS

LORD OF THE BASE PATHS

The baseline belongs to me.

—TY COBB

The game, as practiced by Cobb, was a ceremony of deceit and brutal recklessness. . . . Winning was necessary for him no matter what he did.

—JIMMY CANNON

Cobb lived off the field as though he wished to live forever. He lived on the field as though it was his last day.

—BRANCH RICKEY

I just got to be first—all the time.

—TY COBB

I was like a steel spring with a growing and dangerous flaw in it. If it is wound too tight or has the slightest weak point, the spring will fly apart and then it is done for.

—TY COBB

He was possessed by the Furies.

—BOZEMAN BULGER

If you put the ball on the outside where Cobb likes it, he will drop it into left field. Keep it inside and he is liable to kill your first baseman. About the best way to fool him is to get the ball up there faster than he can get his bat around.

—WALTER JOHNSON

Every great batter works on the theory that the pitcher is more afraid of him than he is of the pitcher.

—TY COBB

28

Ty Cobb, sliding into third—Jimmy Austin is the fielder—in a
1910 game against New York, was feared around the league
for his spikes-flying brand of play. White Sox catcher Ray
Schalk said, "The one thing we didn't want to do against Cobb
was get him mad."

*I know that a lot of people didn't like him, but that was because
of the way he played ball. When he put on that uniform he was a
different person. It became a blood war and he was determined to
beat the fire out of you.*

                —JOE SEWELL, Hall-of-Fame infielder

*I have observed that baseball is not unlike a war, and when you
come right down to it, we batters are the heavy artillery.*

                —TY COBB

This great athlete seems to have understood early in his profes-sional career that in the competition of baseball, just as in war, defensive strategy never has produced ultimate victory and, as a consequence, he maintained an offensive posture to the end of his baseball days.

—GENERAL DOUGLAS MACARTHUR

A ball bat is a wondrous weapon.

—TY COBB

I had to fight all my life to survive. They were all against me and tried every dirty trick to cut me down. But I beat the bastards and left them in the ditch.

—TY COBB

Perhaps Cobb is the least popular player who ever lived. And why? Whether you like or dislike this young fellow, you must con-cede him one virtue: what he has won, he has taken by might of his own play.

—HEYWOOD BROUN

The redoubtable Tyrus Raymond Cobb, sharp of mind and spike, is dead. It would take a long parade of superlatives to re-enact his career, for his talents were of unmatched variety. . . . It is not for us to say that his aggressive preemption of the basepaths was or was not in keeping with the book. We'll leave that to the untiring tongues of grandstand umpires. Of Ty Cobb let it be said simply that he was the world's greatest ballplayer.

—New York *Herald Tribune* editorial, the
morning after Cobb's death on July 17, 1961

BALL PARK CHATTER

Baseball is in its infancy.

—CHARLES EBBETS, president of the Brooklyn
Dodgers (1909)

It is, as a rule, a man's own business how he spends his money. But nevertheless we wish to call attention to the fact that many men do so in a very unwise manner. A very glaring instance of this among baseball players is the recent evil tendency to purchase and maintain automobiles. Put the money away, boys, where it will be safe. You don't need these automobiles. That money will look mighty good later on in life. Think it over, boys.

—*Baseball Magazine* editorial (1914)

I have never known a day when I didn't learn something new about this game.

—CONNIE MACK

You can't hit what you can't see.

—PING BODIE, returning to the dugout after being struck out by Walter Johnson

He's got a gun concealed about his person. They can't tell me he throws them balls with his arm.

—RING LARDNER, on Walter Johnson

Ballplayers are peculiar beings. First, they are caught young, as a rule; second, they are spoiled by overmuch praise if they make good; third, they have about twenty-two hours a day to think about themselves and their troubles, to nurse grievances, and to develop peculiar turns of mind.

—HUGH S. FULLERTON (1916)

Hits are my bread and butter.

—OSSIE VITT, Tigers infielder

He threw a spitball—I think that ball disintegrated on the way to the plate and the catcher put it back together again. I swear, when it went past the plate it was just the spit went by.

—SAM CRAWFORD, Hall-of-Fame outfielder, on the legendary spitter of White Sox right-hander Ed Walsh

Oh, those bases on balls!

—GEORGE STALLINGS, Braves manager, suggesting his epitaph

Although he is a bad fielder he is also a very poor infielder.

—RING LARDNER, on an unnamed player

31

Cy Young won more games—511—and worked in more innings—
7,377—than any other pitcher in baseball history. "On with the
tribute, let garlands be flung. . . . Here's to the king of them
all, Denton Young"—Grantland Rice.

Connie Mack, manager of the Philadelphia A's from 1901 to 1950: "Born in the Lincoln Administration, and still staggering through Eisenhower—he was like a tree with initials on it from the Garden of Eden" —Wilfrid Sheed.

These are the saddest of possible words—
Tinker to Evers to Chance.
Trio of Bear Cubs and fleeter than birds—
Tinker to Evers to Chance.
Ruthlessly pricking our gonfalon bubble,
Making a Giant hit into a double,
Words that are weighty with nothing but trouble—
Tinker to Evers to Chance.

> —FRANKLIN P. ADAMS. New York *Mail* (1910), immortalizing the Cubs' double play combination of shortstop Joe Tinker, second baseman Johnny Evers, and first baseman Frank Chance.

Nothing on earth is more depressing than an old baseball writer.
—RING LARDNER

The Pope for religion, O'Loughlin for baseball. Both are infallible.

> —SILK O'LOUGHLIN, umpire

Let me tell you something, son,
Before you get much older,
You cannot hit the ball, my friend,
With your bat upon your shoulder.

> —BILL BYRON, taunting a batter who'd just struck out. Byron, the "Singing Umpire," was known to ridicule players with his verses and songs.

I ain't afraid to tell the world that it don't take school stuff to help a fellow play ball.

> —SHOELESS JOE JACKSON, White Sox right fielder

He had larceny in his heart, but his feet were honest.

> —BUGS BAER, on plodding base runner Ping Bodie

When you're on a sleeper at night, take your pocketbook and put it in a sock under your pillow. That way, the next morning you won't forget your pocketbook, 'cause you'll be looking for your sock.

> —PING BODIE, advising a rookie

The game of baseball is a clean, straight game, and it summons to its presence everybody who enjoys clean, straight athletics.

> —WILLIAM HOWARD TAFT (1910)

THE BLACK SOX SCANDAL

"Who is he, anyhow, an actor?"
"No."
"A dentist?"
" . . . No, he's a gambler." Gatsby hesitated, then added coolly: "He's the man who fixed the World Series back in 1919."
"Fixed the World Series?" I repeated.
The idea staggered me. I remembered, of course, that the World Series had been fixed in 1919, but if I had thought of it at all I would have thought of it as a thing that merely happened, *the end of some inevitable chain. It never occurred to me that one man could start to play with the faith of fifty million people—with the singlemindedness of a burglar blowing a safe.*
"How did he happen to do that?" I asked after a minute.
"He just saw the opportunity."
"Why isn't he in jail?"
"They can't get him, old sport. He's a smart man."

> —F. SCOTT FITZGERALD, *The Great Gatsby*

Eight members of the 1919 Chicago White Sox were accused of conspiring with gamblers to throw games in that year's World Series. "Benedict Arnolds! Betrayers of American boyhood, not to mention American Girlhood and American Womanhood and American Hoodhood."—Nelson Algren.

I think we can put it in the bag!

> —CHICK GANDIL, White Sox first baseman,
> offering to throw the 1919 series with the help
> of some teammates

YOUNG BOY: *Say it ain't so, Joe. Say it ain't so.*
JOE JACKSON: *Yes, kid, I'm afraid it is.*
YOUNG BOY: *Well, I never would have thought it.*

> —Conversation that supposedly took place
> outside a Chicago courtroom after Joe Jackson
> testified to a 1920 grand jury on his part in the
> Series fix

I've lived a thousand years in the last twelve months. . . . Now I've lost everything, job, reputation, everything. My friends all bet on the Sox. I knew it, but I couldn't tell them. I had to double-cross them. I'm through with baseball. I'm going to lose myself if I can and start life over again.

> —EDDIE CICOTTE, White Sox right-hander
> (1920)

I'd give a million dollars to undo what I've done.

> —EDDIE CICOTTE

Regardless of the verdict of juries, no player that throws a ball game; no player that undertakes or promises to throw a ball game; no player that sits in a conference with a bunch of crooked players and gamblers where the ways and means of throwing games are planned and discussed and does not promptly tell his club about it, will ever play professional baseball.

> —KENESAW MOUNTAIN LANDIS, commissioner
> of baseball, declaring that the eight White Sox
> players—Eddie Cicotte, Happy Felsch, Chick
> Gandil, Joe Jackson, Fred McMullin, Swede
> Risberg, Buck Weaver and Lefty Williams—
> would not be allowed to play organized
> baseball even though a 1921 grand jury failed
> to indict them

We do not trust cashiers half so much, or diplomats, or police-men, or physicians, as we trust an outfielder or a shortstop. The light which beats upon him would do very well for a throne. The one thing which he is not called—many things as he may be called for his blunders—is sneak or traitor. The man at the bat, cheer him or hoot at him as we may, is supposed to be doing his best. . . . All may be fair in love and war, but in sport nothing is fair but the rules.

—The Nation (1920)

3
BABE

O AT THE heart of Babe Ruth's accomplishment was an idea. In 1920 he hit 54 home runs; only one other *team* hit as many as 50 that year. But it was not just that Ruth was the first to explore the possibilities of the long ball; it was the way he did it. His life was as heroic at the dinner table and in the boudoir as it was on the ball field, and the people loved it. No other ballplayer before or since has so moved the public with his personality, his extraordinary talents, his genius.

The Ruth is mighty and shall prevail.
—HEYWOOD BROUN

He was a parade all by himself, a burst of dazzle and jingle. Santa Claus drinking his whiskey straight and groaning with a bellyache caused by gluttony. . . . Babe Ruth made the music that his joyous years danced to in a continuous party. . . . What Babe Ruth is comes down, one generation handing it to the next, as a national heirloom.
—JIMMY CANNON

You know, I saw it all happen, from beginning to end. But sometimes I still can't believe what I saw: this nineteen-year-old kid, crude, poorly educated, only lightly brushed by the social veneer we call civilization, gradually transformed into the idol of American youth and the symbol of baseball the world over—a man loved by more people and with an intensity of feeling that perhaps has never been equaled before or since. I saw a man transformed from a human being into something pretty close to a god.

—HARRY HOOPER, teammate at Boston

It's a gift.

—BABE RUTH

In lashing at the ball, Ruth put his big body back of the smash with as perfect timing as we have ever seen. There was no hurried motion, no quick swinging, no overanxiety to connect. It all happened with the concentrated serenity of great power under perfect control.

—GRANTLAND RICE

That's the first thing I can remember about him—the sound when he'd get a hold of one. It was just different—that's all.

—LARRY GARDNER, teammate at Boston

It wasn't just that he hit more home runs than anybody else, he hit them better, higher, farther, with more theatrical timing and a more flamboyant flourish. Nobody could strike out like Babe Ruth. Nobody circled the bases with the same pigeon-toed, mincing majesty.

—RED SMITH

It was impossible to watch him at bat without experiencing an emotion. I have seen hundreds of ballplayers at the plate, and none of them managed to convey the message of impending doom to a pitcher that Babe Ruth did with the cock of his head, the position of his legs, and the little gentle waving of the bat, feathered in his two big paws.

—PAUL GALLICO

All I can tell 'em is pick a good one and sock it. I get back to the dugout and they ask me what it was I hit and I tell 'em I don't know except it looked good.

—BABE RUTH

I was listed as an incorrigible, and I guess I was. Looking back on my early boyhood, I honestly don't remember being aware of the difference between right and wrong.

> —BABE RUTH

He had the happy faculty of wearing the world as a loose garment.

> —TOM MEANY, sportswriter

REPORTER: *What's it like to room with Babe Ruth?*
PING BODIE: *I don't room with Babe. I room with his suitcase.*

Hot as hell, ain't it, Prez?

> —BABE RUTH to Warren G. Harding, upon being introduced on a sweltering hot day in Washington. Some years later, in 1929, Ruth was asked if he thought it was right that he was making more money than the President. "Why not?" said the Babe. "I had a better year than he did."

Babe Ruth and Old Jack Dempsey
Both Sultans of the Swat,
One hits where other people are—
The other where they're not.

> —JOHN LARDNER

Babe sets a single season mark with his sixtieth home run of 1927. "Once he had that fifty-nine, that number sixty was sure as the setting sun. A more determined athlete than George Herman Ruth never lived"—Paul Gallico.

He did, with the home run, things that were incredible and that seemed impossible; in fact, [they] were impossible to everyone else.

—FRANK LANE, baseball executive

Anytime that fellow was involved in anything, good, bad, or indifferent, everybody paid attention. You could love him, hate him, or be neutral, but you couldn't ignore him. There never was such a personality on a ball field. Talking about him can never do him justice. You had to be there, you had to see for yourself.

—JOE SEWELL, teammate at New York

The door opened and it was God himself who walked into the room, straight from His glittering throne, God dressed in a camel's hair polo coat and camel's hair cap, God with a flat nose and little piggy eyes and a big grin, and a fat, black cigar sticking out of the side of it.

—PAUL GALLICO on Ruth's legendary hospital visit to ailing Johnny Sylvester. It's said that Ruth promised to hit a home run for the boy that day—and did.

I have only one superstition. I make sure to touch all the bases when I hit a home run.

—BABE RUTH

A rabbit didn't have to think to know what to do to dodge a dog. . . . The same kind of instinct told Babe Ruth what to do and where to be.

—SAMMY VICK, teammate at New York

Born? Hell, Babe Ruth wasn't born. The sonofabitch fell from a tree.

—JOE DUGAN, teammate at New York

Don't tell me about Ruth; I've seen what he did to people. I've seen them, fans, driving miles in open wagons through the prairies of Oklahoma to see him in exhibition games as we headed north in the spring. I've seen them: kids, men, women, worshippers all, hoping to get his name on a torn, dirty piece of paper, or hoping for a grunt of recognition when they said, "Hi ya, Babe." He never let them down; not once. He was the greatest crowd pleaser of them all.

—WAITE HOYT, teammate at Boston and New York

The fans would rather see me hit one homer to right than three doubles to left.

—BABE RUTH

If I make a home run every time I bat, they think I'm all right. If I don't, they think they can call me anything they like.

—BABE RUTH

He'd hit 'em so high that everyone on the field thought he had a chance to get it. They'd all try to get under it to make the catch, and it looked like a union meetin'.

—CASEY STENGEL, describing a Babe Ruth pop-up

Ruth filled the parks by developing the home run into a hit of exciting elegance. For almost two decades he battered fences with such regularity that baseball's basic structure was eventually pounded into a different shape.

—LEE ALLEN, baseball historian

Wives of ballplayers, when they teach their children their prayers, should instruct them to say: "God bless Mommy, God bless Daddy, God bless Babe Ruth!" Babe has upped daddy's paycheck by fifteen to forty percent.

—WAITE HOYT

The only real game in the world, I think, is baseball. . . . You've got to start way down, at the bottom, when you're six or seven years old. You can't wait until you're fifteen or sixteen. You've got to let it grow up with you, and if you're successful and you try hard enough, you're bound to come out on top, just like these boys have come to the top now.

—BABE RUTH, in his 1948 farewell speech at Yankee Stadium

Hello, Mr. Mack. The termites have got me.

—An ailing Babe Ruth to Connie Mack, not long before Ruth's death from cancer on August 16, 1948

With vim and verve he walloped the curve
From Texas to Duluth
Which is no small task,
And I rise to ask:
Was there ever a guy like Ruth?
—John Kieran

JOE DUGAN *(suffering in the heat at Ruth's funeral): I'd give a hundred dollars for a beer.*
WAITE HOYT: *So would the Babe.*

Some twenty years ago, I stopped talking about the Babe for the simple reason that I realized that those who had never seen him didn't believe me.

—TOMMY HOLMES, sportswriter

I guess I just liked the game.

—BABE RUTH

4
BUSTING DOWN THE FENCES: 1921–35

O THE BLACK SOX SCANDAL rocked the baseball world, and to some it looked as if the game might not recover. But baseball has a great capacity for rejuvenating itself. An Illinois judge named Kenesaw Mountain Landis was appointed the first commissioner of baseball, and his stern, moralistic hand helped restore public confidence in the game. Meanwhile, on the field a revolution was taking place. The likes of Babe Ruth, Rogers Hornsby, and later Lou Gehrig and Jimmie Foxx brought out fans in record numbers with a new, exciting brand of ball powered by the home run.

DYNASTY (PART I)

The secret of success as a pitcher lies in getting a job with the Yankees.

—WAITE HOYT (1927)

45

My idea of a good ballgame is one where the Yankees have a thirteen-run lead in the top of the ninth with two out and two strikes on the hitter.

> —COLONEL JACOB RUPPERT, owner of the
> Yankees

What's the matter with you, Hoyt? You win all your games one to nothing or two to one. Pennock, Bush, Shawkey, those fellows— they win nine or ten to one. Why don't you win some like that?

> —JACOB RUPPERT, admonishing Waite Hoyt

Baseball is not supported by civic pride. It's supported by interest in winners, a desire to see them perform or the hope that they'll get licked. . . . Practically nobody will go, whatever his civic pride, to see a tail-ender.

> —TILLINGHAST L'HOMMEDIEU HUSTON, co-
> owner of the Yankees until selling out to
> Ruppert

Championship baseball teams are not founded on bats. They're built on a backbone of catching, pitching, a second base combination and a center fielder.

> —CARL MAYS, Yankees right-hander

A catcher must want to catch. He must make up his mind that it isn't the terrible job it is painted, and that he isn't going to say almost every day, "Why, oh why, with so many other positions in baseball, did I take up this one?"

> —BILL DICKEY, Yankees catcher

The first commandment is observation. Look around, notice the little quirks in the batter, and notice your own quirks. Your doctor never stops learning. The great pitcher imitates him.

> —HERB PENNOCK, Yankees left-hander

A manager has his cards dealt to him, and he must play them.

> —MILLER HUGGINS, Yankee manager, once
> described by Gerald Holland as "the skinny
> little scrap of a fellow who did not seem to be
> able to find a uniform small enough to fit him."

Although he was one of the game's greatest sluggers, Lou Gehrig was overshadowed for much of his career by Babe Ruth. As Franklin P. Adams put it, he was "the guy who hit all those homers the year Ruth set the record."

Gee, they're big, aren't they?

> —LLOYD WANER, Pirates rookie, to his brother,
> Paul, as they watched the power-laden 1927
> Yankees take batting practice before that year's
> World Series. New York swept Pittsburgh.

The ballplayer who loses his head, who can't keep cool, is worse than no ballplayer at all.

> —LOU GEHRIG

Lou was the kind of boy if you had a son he's the kind of person you'd like your son to be.

> —SAM JONES, Gehrig's teammate

Gehrig never learned that a ballplayer couldn't be good every day.

> —HANK GOWDY, Braves catcher

Playing for the Yankees calls for being the same kind of gentleman who would work in a bank.

> —JOE MCCARTHY, who became Yankees
> manager in 1931

Joe, I'm out of the lineup. I'm just not doing the team any good.

> —LOU GEHRIG to Joe McCarthy, taking
> himself out of the Yankee lineup, May 2, 1939,
> after playing in 2,130 consecutive games

Fans, for the past two weeks you have been reading about what a bad break I got. Yet today I consider myself the luckiest man on the face of the earth. . . . I might have had a tough break, but I have an awful lot to live for.

> —LOU GEHRIG, addressing the crowd at a day
> in his honor at Yankee Stadium, July 4, 1939.
> Two years later Gehrig died from amyotrophic
> lateral sclerosis, a rare kind of paralysis.

BALL PARK CHATTER

When you put the ball between your thumb and forefinger, you can hear a rabbit's pulsebeat.

> —WESTBROOK PEGLER, on the new, "live"
> baseball introduced in 1920

Baseball is the national game, not just a diversion for Manhattanites.

        —*The Sporting News*, deploring the all–New York 1921 World Series. Because the Polo Grounds was at that time the home park for both the Giants and Yankees, the entire series was played within the borough of Manhattan.

It makes no difference where I go or what happens, so long as I can play the full nine.

        —ROGERS HORNSBY

Anybody who says he isn't nervous or excited in a World Series is either crazy or a liar.

        —ROGERS HORNSBY

He was frank to the point of being cruel, and subtle as a belch.

        —LEE ALLEN, on Rogers Hornsby

His career typifies the heights to which dramatic talent may carry a man in America if only he has the foresight not to go on the stage.

        —HEYWOOD BROUN, on Kenesaw Mountain Landis

Sluggers (left to right) Rogers Hornsby, Hack Wilson, Al Simmons and Jimmie Foxx shake hands before the 1929 World Series. "Guys who can field you can shake out of any old tree. Give me a guy who can hit"—Rogers Hornsby.

It is hard for fans to believe a guy named Cohen can play ball.

—ANDY COHEN, Giants infielder

Wee Willie Keeler,
You have journeyed West;
Just an old Oriole
Flown to his rest.

Wee Willie Keeler,
Smallest of them all;
But in height of manhood
You were mountains tall.

—WALTER TRUMBULL, commemorating the
death in 1923 of the five-foot four-and-a-half-
inch Keeler, one of batting's earliest (and best)
craftsmen

It's not the bat that counts. It's the guy who's wheeling it.

—PAUL WANER, Pirates outfielder

We cannot imagine . . . anything more worldly or unreligious in
the way of employment than the playing of professional baseball as
it is played today.

—PENNSYLVANIA SUPREME COURT (1927)

There is much less drinking now than there was before 1927,
because I quit drinking on May 24, 1927.

—RABBIT MARANVILLE, Hall-of-Fame infielder

You know, they say money talks. But the only thing it ever says
to me is good-bye.

—PAUL WANER

I've never played drunk; hungover yes, but never drunk.

—HACK WILSON. The Cubs slugger was
renowned for his drinking. Warren Brown
joked that "Wilson was a high ball hitter on the
field, and off it."

I am quite sure that statistics will show that the greatest number
of successes have been scored by those [ballplayers] who have led
moderately dirty lives.

—W. O. McGEEHAN

Pepper Martin, the Cardinals' center fielder, slides into third during a game at Sportsman's Park. "When (Pepper) ran he took flight, wings beating, beak splitting the wind, and when he stole a base he swooped down on it with a predator's headlong dive"—Red Smith.

The tradition of professional baseball always has been agreeably free of chivalry. The rule is "Do anything you can get away with."
                    —HEYWOOD BROUN

> *They give a rookie fifteen days,*
> * To gamble with his fate;*
> *For each who makes the grade and stays,*
> * A dozen get the gate.*
>   —PAT PATTEN (1930)

BABE RUTH (after being called out on strikes): *There's forty thousand people here who know that last one was a ball, tomato head!*

UMPIRE BABE PINELLI: *Maybe so, but mine is the only opinion that counts.*

> *I'm holding my breath*
> *I'm afraid to speak*
> *About the Cubs*
> *And their winning streak.*

51

It looks too close
To be bragging around
'Bout our pennant hopes
Lest they tumble down.
I'll just sit quiet
Never utter a word
For they may finish second
Or possibly . . . third.

> —LORD REGEIRKSEL (1929). The Cubs, it
> should be added, won the pennant that year.

Charlie Gehringer is in a rut. He hits .350 on opening day and
stays there all season.

> —LEFTY GOMEZ

Jimmie Foxx wasn't scouted, he was trapped.

> —LEFTY GOMEZ

Lonny Frey is an infielder with only one weakness: batted balls.

> —Popular joke about the early '30s Dodger
> shortstop

The Dodgers have Del Bissonette
No meal has he ever missed yet.
The question that rises
Is one that surprises:
Who paid for all Del Bissonette?

> —L. H. Addington

Brooklyn? Is Brooklyn still in the league?

> —BILL TERRY, Giants manager, spring 1934.
> Terry's words came back to haunt him as the
> lowly Dodgers beat the Giants the last two
> games of the season to deprive them of the
> pennant.

The whole art of pitching is in the wrist.

> —CARL HUBBELL

He could throw strikes at midnight.

> —BILLY HERMAN, Hall-of-Fame second
> baseman, on Carl Hubbell

He could throw a cream puff through a battleship.

—JOHNNY FREDERICK, Dodger outfielder, on teammate Dazzy Vance

He could throw a lamb chop past a wolf.

—BUGS BAER, on Lefty Grove

THE GASHOUSE GANG

Swarming up from the Texas wheat fields, the Georgia cotton lands, the West Virginia coal mines, the Oklahoma cow ranges and the Ozark farms, the Gas Housers redramatized for the public that old traditional story about the talent of common men. They fit the historic pattern of the American success story, the legend of the country boy who, on native wit and vitality, crashes through, clear up to the top.

—LLOYD LEWIS on the 1934 St. Louis Cardinals

Dizzy Dean (right) pitched a three-hitter in the opener of a 1934 doubleheader; brother Paul (left) followed with a no-hitter. "If I'd known Paul was going to pitch a no-hitter," said Dizzy, "I'd a pitched one too."

REPORTER: *Mr. Martin, how did you learn to run the way you do?*

PEPPER MARTIN: *Well sir, I grew up in Oklahoma and out there, once you start running there ain't nothing to stop you.*

DOCTOR (examining Dizzy Dean's injured toe): *This toe is fractured.*

DIZZY DEAN: *Fractured, hell! The damn thing's broken.*

I know why they threw that stuff at me. What I can't figure out is why they brought it to the ball park in the first place.

> —JOE MEDWICK, Cardinals outfielder, after
> Tiger fans pelted him with fruit, bottles and
> trash during the 1934 World Series

You don't like your players or dislike them. . . . There's no room for sentiment in baseball if you want to win.

> —FRANKIE FRISCH, Cardinals player-manager

There's nothing tough about playing third. All a guy needs is a strong arm and a strong chest.

> —FRANKIE FRISCH, who played both second
> and third during his career

Dizzy Dean realized the American dream at a time when most Americans had abandoned it. The country wanted entertainment more than it wanted inspiration, and he filled the need.

> —Anonymous sportswriter (1934)

Old Diz knows the King's English. And not only that. I also know the Queen is English.

> —DIZZY DEAN

X RAYS OF DEAN'S HEAD SHOW NOTHING

> —Newspaper headline after Dizzy was knocked
> in the head during the 1934 Series

If you can do it, it ain't braggin'.

> —DIZZY DEAN

54

Where do folks get off criticizing my grammar? I only went up to the second grade, and if I'd gone up to the third, I'd 'a passed my old man.

—DIZZY DEAN

It don't make no difference how you say it, just say it in a way that makes sense. Did you ever meet anybody in your life who didn't know what "ain't" means?

—DIZZY DEAN

Some people who don't say "ain't," ain't eating.

—DIZZY DEAN

I couldn't break a pane of glass.

—DIZZY DEAN, on the sore arm that crippled his pitching career

I ain't what I used to be, but who the hell is?

—DIZZY DEAN, late in his career

It's pretty nice for an ol' Arkansas cotton picker to be up here with these city boys. The good Lord was good to me. He gave me a strong body, a good right arm and a weak mind.

—DIZZY DEAN, at his induction into the Hall of Fame in 1953

I may not have been the greatest pitcher ever, but I was amongst 'em.

—DIZZY DEAN

THE INVISIBLE MEN

There's a couple of million dollars worth of baseball talent on the loose, ready for the big leagues, yet unsigned by any major league. There are pitchers who would win 20 games a season . . . and outfielders [who] could hit .350, infielders who could win recognition as stars, and there's at least one catcher who at this writing is probably superior to Bill Dickey, Josh Gibson. Only one thing is keeping them out of the big leagues, the pigmentation of their skin. They happen to be colored.

—SHIRLEY POVICH, sportswriter (1941)

The 1921 Chicago American Giants (above); some of the 1932 Pittsburgh Crawfords (below). "I am an invisible man. . . . I am invisible, understand, simply because people refuse to see me. Like the bodiless heads you see sometimes in circus sideshows, it is as though I have been surrounded by mirrors of hard, distorting glass. When they approach me they see only my surroundings, themselves, or figments of their imagination—indeed, everything and anything except me"—Ralph Ellison.

James "Cool Papa" Bell, star center fielder in the Negro leagues. "Cool Papa Bell was so fast he could get out of bed, turn out the lights across the room, and be back in bed under the covers before the lights went out"—Josh Gibson.

There is a catcher that any big league club would like to buy for $200,000. His name is Gibson. . . . He can do everything. He hits the ball a mile. And he catches so easy he might as well be in a rocking chair. Throws like a rifle.

      —WALTER JOHNSON

A homer a day will boost my pay.

      —JOSH GIBSON

We was playin' the Homestead Grays in the city of Pitchburgh. Josh comes up in the last of the ninth with a man on and us a run behind. Well, he hit one. The Grays waited around and waited around, but finally the empire rules it ain't comin' down. So we win. The next day, we was disputin' the Grays in Philadelphia when here come a ball outta the sky right in the glove of the Grays' center fielder. The empire made the only possible call. "You're out, boy!" he says to Josh. "Yesterday, in Pitchburgh."

      —SATCHEL PAIGE

Let me tell you about Cool Papa Bell. One time he hit a line drive right past my ear. I turned around and saw the ball hit his ass sliding into second.

      —SATCHEL PAIGE

A lot of pitchers have a fastball, but a very, very few—Feller, Grove, Johnson, a couple of others besides Satchel—have had that

57

little extra juice. . . . When it's fast, it will hop a little at the end of the line. Beyond that, it tends to disappear. Yes, disappear. I've heard about Satchel throwing pitches that wasn't hit but that never showed up in the catcher's mitt, nevertheless. They say the catcher, the umpire and the bat boys looked all over for that ball, but it was gone. Now how do you account for that?

> —BIZ MACKEY, catcher for the Baltimore Elite Giants

It got so I could nip frosting off a cake with my fastball.

> —SATCHEL PAIGE. Once asked how his fastball would do against Josh Gibson, Satchel said, "If he can't see it, he can't hit it."

Just take the ball and throw it where you want to. Throw strikes. Home plate don't move.

> —SATCHEL PAIGE

With women, it's like this: I'm not married, but I'm in great demand.

> —SATCHEL PAIGE

I've majored in geography, transportation and people. Ah been a travelin' man.

> —SATCHEL PAIGE

Satchel Paige is above race and beyond prejudice. He is interracial and universal.

> —BILL VEECK. In 1953 Paige, at age forty-seven, pitched in fifty-seven ballgames for the Veeck-owned St. Louis Browns. He had been admitted into the majors only five years earlier. Once Casey Stengel, seeing Paige warming up in the bullpen for the Browns, warned his players, "Get the runs now! Father Time is coming!"

Age is a question of mind over matter. If you don't mind, it doesn't matter.

> —SATCHEL PAIGE

How old would you be if you didn't know how old you was?

> —SATCHEL PAIGE

Satchel Paige, shown here in 1942, was perhaps the greatest pitcher of his day. In the mid-thirties a young minor leaguer named Joe DiMaggio faced Paige in an exhibition game. An ecstatic Yankee scout wired New York the result: "DiMaggio all we hoped he'd be. Hit Satch one for four."

Listen, if I had it to do all over again, I would. I had more fun and seen more places with less money than if I was Rockefeller.

—SATCHEL PAIGE

I have no ill feeling about never having had the opportunity to play in the big leagues. You know, they used to call me the black Lloyd Waner. I used to think about that a lot. He was on the other side of town in Pittsburgh making twelve thousand dollars a year, and I didn't have enough money to go home on. I had to borrow bus fare to come home. . . . But that was yesterday. There's no use in me having bitterness in my heart this late in life about what's gone by. I can say I contributed something.

—JIMMIE CRUTCHFIELD, Pittsburgh Crawfords outfielder

There's nothing greater for a human being than to get his body to react to all the things one does on a ball field. It's as good as sex; it's as good as music; it fills you up. Waste no tears for me. I didn't come along too early. I was right on time.

—BUCK O'NEIL, recalling his days as an infielder for the Kansas City Monarchs

5
A TIME TO REMEMBER: 1936–50

○ IT'S SAID that some ballplayers breaking into the majors today do not know who Jackie Robinson was. Similarly, millions of young television watchers know Joe DiMaggio only from his commercials. This would be dispiriting were it not for the memories and film and, perhaps more importantly, the record. Among other things, Jackie Robinson stole home nineteen times, once in the World Series. In 1941 Joe DiMaggio hit safely in fifty-six consecutive games, paused a game, then hit safely in another sixteen straight. No matter what, you can't take that away from them—you can't take that away.

AMAZING GRACE

I'd like to thank the good Lord for making me a Yankee.
—JOE DIMAGGIO

It has been aptly said that while Ruth was the Home Run King, Gehrig was the Crown Prince. Joe DiMaggio must therefore have been heir apparent.
—CONNIE MACK

When Joe DiMaggio was asked why he always played so hard, he said, "Because there is always some kid who may be seeing me for the first or last time. I owe him my best."

If you saw him play, you'll never forget him. No one ran with such unhurried grace. His gifts as an athlete were marvelous because they were subdued. Here was an outfielder who followed a fly ball with a deft serenity as though his progress had been plotted by a choreographer concerned only with the defeat of awkwardness.

—JIMMY CANNON

The phrase "off with the crack of the bat," while romantic, is really meaningless, since the outfielder should be in motion long before he hears the sound of the ball meeting the bat.

—JOE DIMAGGIO

It used to amaze me how graceful he was in the outfield, how stylish he was in going after a ball. He never seemed to be in a hurry, but he was always there.

—MONTE IRVIN, Hall-of-Fame outfielder

There is no trick to catching a ball in the open field. . . . The test of an outfielder's skill comes when he has to go against the fence to make a catch.

—JOE DIMAGGIO

You saw him standing there and you knew you had a pretty damn good chance to win the baseball game.

—RED RUFFING, teammate at New York

He was a guy who knew he was the greatest ballplayer in America, and he was proud of it. He knew what the press and the fans and the kids expected of him, and he was always trying to live up to that image. . . . He knew he was Joe DiMaggio, and he knew what that meant to the country.

—LEFTY GOMEZ, teammate at New York

I can remember a reporter asking for a quote, and I didn't know what a quote was. I thought it was some kind of soft drink.

—JOE DIMAGGIO

A ballplayer's got to be kept hungry to become a big leaguer. That's why no boy from a rich family ever made the big leagues.

—JOE DIMAGGIO

The game of baseball was simple to him, and he never attempted to make it complicated. . . . He never pressed when he didn't have to and this was a beautiful skill. It was this that made him exceptional, this stately reserve, as though the desperation of the competition should remain a private matter.

—JIMMY CANNON

I'm a ballplayer, not an actor.

—JOE DIMAGGIO

I was always conscious of the other guy. Usually the other guy was Joe DiMaggio.

—TED WILLIAMS

The Yankees have a guy named DiMaggio. Sometimes a fellow gets a little tired writing about DiMaggio. A fellow thinks, "There must be some other ballplayer in the world worth mentioning." But there isn't really, not worth mentioning in the same breath with DiMaggio.

—RED SMITH (1948)

There's no skill involved. Just go up there and swing at the ball.

—JOE DIMAGGIO

I'm responsible for Joe DiMaggio's success. They never knew how he could go back on a ball until I pitched.

—LEFTY GOMEZ

All I ever saw of Joe on the field was the back of his uniform. I wouldn't have known what he looked like except we roomed together.

—LEFTY GOMEZ

I no longer have it, and when baseball is no longer fun, it is no longer a game.

—JOE DIMAGGIO, announcing his retirement
from baseball after the 1951 season

THE KID

All I want out of life is that when I walk down the street folks will say, "There goes the greatest hitter who ever lived."

—TED WILLIAMS

Ted Williams was standing around a batting cage with some other players in the spring of 1938 when a Red Sox player told him, "Wait until you see Jimmie Foxx hit." Then only a teenager and not yet a major leaguer, Williams replied, "Wait until Jimmie Foxx sees me hit."

It may be that, compared to such managers' dreams as the manifestly classy Joe DiMaggio and the always helpful Stan Musial, Williams was an icy star. But of all team sports, baseball, with its graceful intermittences of action, its immense and tranquil field sparsely settled with poised men in white, its dispassionate mathematics, seems to be best suited to accommodate, and be ornamented by, a loner. It is an essentially lonely game. No other player visible to my generation concentrated within himself so much of the sport's poignance, so assiduously refined his natural skills, so constantly brought to the plate that intensity of competence that crowds the throat with joy.

—JOHN UPDIKE

I've found that you don't need to wear a necktie if you can hit.

—TED WILLIAMS

But I'll tell you this—I made up my mind a long time ago not to get too excited, no matter which way the crowd goes. I get paid for playing left field and for hitting that baseball. I am not a participant in a popularity contest.

—TED WILLIAMS

Williams' career, in contrast [to Babe Ruth's], has been a series of failures except for his averages. He flopped in the only World Series he ever played in [1946] when he batted only .200. He flopped in the playoff game with Cleveland in 1948. He flopped in the final game of the 1949 season with the pennant hinging on the outcome. . . . It has always been Williams' records first, the team second, and the Sox non-winning record is proof of that.

—HUCK FINNEGAN, Boston *American*

By the time the press of Boston has completed its daily treatment of Theodore S. Williams, there is no room in the papers for anything but two sticks of agate type about Truman and housing, and one column for the last Boston girl to be murdered on a beach.

—JOHN LARDNER

Nuts to this baseball. I'd sooner be a fireman.

—TED WILLIAMS

We have three big leagues now. There's the American, the National, and then there's Ted Williams.

—MICKEY HARRIS, teammate at Boston

ROOKIE PITCHER: *How should I pitch Ted Williams? Can I pitch him low?*

LOU BOUDREAU: *Yeah, you can pitch him low, but as soon as you throw the ball, run and hide behind second base.*

They didn't know whether to pitch me high or pitch me low. They didn't know what to do.

—TED WILLIAMS

For me, Williams is the classic ballplayer of the game on a hot August weekday, before a small crowd, when the only thing at stake is the tissue-thin difference between a thing done well and a thing done ill.

—JOHN UPDIKE

Ballplayers are not born great. They're not born great hitters or pitchers or managers, and luck isn't the big factor. No one has come up with a substitute for hard work. I've never met a great player who didn't have to work harder at learning to play ball than anything else he ever did.

—TED WILLIAMS

And now Boston knows how England felt when it lost India.

—ED LINN, sportswriter, on Ted Williams's 1960 retirement from the Red Sox

BALL PARK CHATTER

REPORTER: *As a pitcher, what do you consider your greatest asset?*

LEFTY GOMEZ: *Fast outfielders.*

I'm throwing just as hard as I ever did. The ball's just not getting there as fast.

—LEFTY GOMEZ, on his pitching problems late in his career

Luke Hamlin is so wild, if he fell off the Brooklyn Bridge, he would not hit the water.

—TOM MEANY, on Dodgers pitcher Luke "Hot Potato" Hamlin

Leo Durocher, fiery manager of the Brooklyn Dodgers, didn't smile much when the game was on. "Show me a good loser," he said, "and I'll show you an idiot."

You ought to play it mean. They ought to hate you on the field.
— WHIT WYATT, Dodgers pitcher

What are we out at the park for except to win? I'd trip my mother. I'll help her up, brush her off, tell her I'm sorry. But Mother don't make it to third.
— LEO DUROCHER

Leo Durocher is a man with an infinite capacity for immediately making a bad thing worse.
— BRANCH RICKEY

I don't have to tell you that every ballplayer's prayers are directed toward New York and a job with the Yankees.
— ROY WEATHERLY, after being traded to the Yankees in 1943

There's something about the Yankee uniform that gets you. I think it's the wool—it itches.
— JOE GALLAGHER, Yankees outfielder

There are only two things a manager needs to know: when to change pitchers and how to get along with your players.
— BUCKY HARRIS, Senators manager

Go up and hit what you see. And if you don't see anything, come on back.
— BUCKY HARRIS, advising his team on how to hit against Bob Feller

No one can tell you how to hit home runs. You either have the natural strength and reflexes, or you don't.

—HANK GREENBERG, Tigers slugger

Rex Barney would be the league's best pitcher if the plate were high and outside.

—BOB COOKE, sportswriter

A pitcher hasn't anything if he hasn't control.

—JOE MCCARTHY

The only way you can get along with newspapermen is to be like Dizzy Dean. Say something one minute and something different the next.

—HANK GREENBERG

REPORTER: *Can baseball survive a world war?*
BILL TERRY: *It can survive anything.*

I honestly feel it would be best for the country to keep baseball going. There will be fewer people unemployed and everybody will work longer hours and harder than ever before. . . . Here is another way of looking at it—if 300 teams use 5,000 or 6,000 players, these players are a definite recreational asset to at least 20,000,000 of their fellow citizens—and that in my judgment is thoroughly worthwhile.

—FRANKLIN D. ROOSEVELT, in 1942 giving the "green light" to baseball to continue operating during the war

To hell with Babe Ruth!

—Rallying cry of Japanese soldiers as they charged American lines during World War II

It is the fat men against the tall men at the annual office picnic.

—FRANK GRAHAM, sportswriter, on the 1945 Cubs-Tigers World Series. Both teams' rosters were thinned by the war, and play was considered well below standard. Assessing the same Series, Warren Brown said, "I don't think either team can win it."

Joe Garagiola starred for the Cards in the '46 World Series, but didn't amount to much as a ballplayer after that. "I'll give you an idea of what kind of team the Pirates were when I was a player," says Ralph Kiner. "Our catcher was Joe Garagiola."

Home run hitters drive Cadillacs; singles hitters drive Fords.
—Ralph Kiner, home run hitter

What's the best way to pitch to Stan Musial? That's easy. Walk him and then try to pick him off first base.
—Joe Garagiola

Nick Etten's glove fields better with Nick Etten out of it.
—Joe Trimble, sportswriter on the poor-fielding Yankees first baseman

Anybody who can't get along with a .400 hitter is crazy.
—Joe McCarthy, asked if he thought he'd have any problems managing Ted Williams at Boston

Bill Dickey is learning me his experience.
—Yogi Berra, in his rookie season

He can't run, he can't hit, he can't throw; all he can do is beat you.
—Popular saying about second baseman Eddie Stanky

The art of hitting is the art of getting your pitch to hit.
—Bobby Brown, Yankees utilityman

69

A pitcher needs two pitches—one they're looking for and one to cross 'em up.

> —WARREN SPAHN. Besides Spahn and Johnny Sain, the '48 Braves were woefully weak on pitching, prompting one wag to remark that the key to a pennant would be a rotation of "Spahn and Sain and two days of rain."

Don't find many faults with the umpire. You can't expect him to be as perfect as you are.

> —JOE McCARTHY

Trade a player a year too early rather than a year too late.

> —BRANCH RICKEY

I'll never quit. They'll have to tear my uniform off.

> —ENOS SLAUGHTER, Cardinals outfielder

On the ball field he is perpetual motion itself. . . . He would run through a brick wall, if necessary, to make a catch, or slide into a pit of ground glass to score a run.

> —ARTHUR DALEY, on Enos Slaughter. Casey Stengel said of Slaughter: "Some of my players think he's a show-off. That's because every time they see him he's running."

Your arm is gone; your legs likewise,
But not your eyes, Mize, not your eyes.

> —DAN PARKER, paying tribute to Johnny Mize after he hit twenty-five homers in 1950 at age thirty-seven

I'm not quitting because I'm too old. I'm quitting because I think the people want me to.

> —CONNIE MACK, retiring from baseball at age eighty-eight

If I were to write my own epitaph it would read, "He loved his God, his home, his country, his fellow men and baseball."

> —CONNIE MACK

Old Pete may have died stone broke, but all the money in the world won't buy you three hundred and seventy-three major league victories. He's got them, forever.

> —JACK SHER, on the death of Grover Cleveland
> Alexander in 1950

JACKIE ROBINSON AND BREAKING THE COLOR BARRIER

It has been exactly twenty years since Jackie Robinson broke the color line in major league baseball. Branch Rickey signed Robinson as an infielder to play at Montreal in the International League in 1946, but it wasn't until early in 1947 that Jackie came to the Dodger training camp to tune up for one of the most dramatic and fruitful steps since the Civil War toward social integration. That Jackie Robinson made full use of the opportunity to break through the big league color line is now so deep in history that many forget how important he and Branch Rickey were to the cause.

> —*Saturday Review* (1967)

All of us, we had to wait for Jackie.

> —JOE BLACK, Dodgers right-hander

Jackie Robinson, described by one writer as "a revolutionist in a baseball suit," signs his 1948 contract with the Dodgers president, Branch Rickey.

JACKIE ROBINSON (at his first meeting with Rickey): *Are you looking for a Negro who is afraid to fight back?*
BRANCH RICKEY: *No. I'm looking for a ballplayer with the guts enough not to fight back.*

The most significant sports story of the century was written into the record books today as baseball took up the cudgel of democracy and an unassuming Negro ascended the heights of excellence to prove the rightness of the experiment. And prove it in the only correct crucible for such an experiment—the crucible of white-hot competition.

> —JOE BOSTIC, New York *Amsterdam News,*
> after Robinson went four for five on his first
> day in organized ball

I'm not concerned with your liking or disliking me. . . . All I ask is that you respect me as a human being.
> —JACKIE ROBINSON

Jackie Robinson is the loneliest man I have ever seen in sports.
> —JIMMY CANNON (1947)

Like a few, very few athletes . . . Robinson did not merely play at center stage. He was center stage; and wherever he walked, center stage moved with him.
> —ROGER KAHN

I do not care if half the league strikes. Those who do will encounter quick retribution. All will be suspended, and I don't care if it wrecks the National League for five years. This is the United States of America and one citizen has as much right to play as another.

> —FORD FRICK, National League President,
> reacting to a threatened strike by some
> Cardinal players in 1947 if Jackie Robinson
> took the field against St. Louis. The Cardinals
> backed down and played.

Thinking about the things that happened, I don't know any other ball player who could have done what he did. To be able to hit with everybody yelling at him. He had to block all that out, block out

Jackie Robinson steals home in the 1955 World Series. Yogi Berra applies the tag too late, while Carl Furillo looks on. "The word for Jackie Robinson is 'unconquerable' " —Red Smith.

everything but this ball that is coming in at a hundred miles an hour. . . . To do what he did has got to be the most tremendous thing I've ever seen in sports.

—PEE WEE REESE, Robinson's teammate

Give me five players like Robinson and a pitcher, and I'll beat any nine-man team in baseball.

—CHARLIE DRESSEN, Dodgers manager

Robinson could hit and bunt and steal and run. He had intimidating skills, and he burned with a dark fire. He wanted passionately to win. . . . He bore the burden of a pioneer and the weight made him more strong. If one can be certain of anything in baseball, it is that we shall not look upon his like again.

—ROGER KAHN

If there is an unfilled obligation in the case of baseball vs. Jackie Robinson, the debt belongs to baseball, which can never pay off in full.

—HAROLD WEISSMAN, sportswriter

Every time I look at my pocketbook, I see Jackie Robinson.
—WILLIE MAYS

he was a classic hero, and like all classic heroes he carried with him one flaw imposed by fate. he was black. as surely as oedipus or any of them, his flaw destroyed him, crippling him, blinding him, killing him at fifty-three as sadly as with oedipus or any of them. . . . by his talents and his forbearance and his flaw baseball was changed forever.

—JOEL OPPENHEIMER, poet

6
THE GOLDEN YEARS: THE '50s

O BASEBALL'S "GOLDEN YEARS" is a subject of much debate among the game's historians. Some say that the tight, highly strategic brand of ball played in the early 1900s was the high point; others argue for the era of Babe Ruth. One can argue persuasively, however, that baseball has never been better than in the '50s, especially the early part. What other era can match the high drama of The Shot Heard 'round the World, the supreme competence of the Mantle-led Yankees, the heroic ardor of the Brooklyn Dodgers? What's more, Willie Mays broke into the major leagues in 1951. That fact alone makes this period incomparable.

THE CENTER FIELDER

I believed when I went on that field that I was on stage.
—WILLIE MAYS

If somebody came up and hit .450, stole 100 bases and performed a miracle in the field every day I'd still look you in the eye and say Willie was better. He could do the five things you have to do to be a

Mickey Mantle and Willie Mays in 1951. "Oh to be a center fielder, a center fielder—and nothing more!"—Philip Roth.

superstar: hit, hit with power, run, throw and field. And he had that other magic ingredient that turns a superstar into a super superstar. He lit up the room when he came in. He was a joy to be around.

—LEO DUROCHER

To watch Mays play was to watch Rembrandt paint or Caruso sing.

—Anonymous sportswriter

I fell in love with him that afternoon. And watching him then, I realized unconsciously that it was about time he arrived on my horizon. . . . He was what it was all about. He was the reason. In my head, there was a notion of the way things ought to happen, but never quite do. Not until Willie came along. And then I could finally sit there and say to myself, Oh, sure, that's it.

—WILLIAM GOLDMAN, screenwriter

My God, look at those hands!

—The first words, according to baseball legend, of the doctor after he delivered Willie Mays

He was something like O for twenty-one the first time I saw him. His first major league hit was a home run off me—and I'll never forgive myself. We might have gotten rid of Willie forever if I'd only struck him out.

—WARREN SPAHN

It's not hard. When I'm not hittin', I don't hit nobody. But when I'm hittin', I hit anybody.

—WILLIE MAYS

It don't make no difference to me what kind of a game it is, I always play it as hard as I can. That's the onliest way I know how to play ball.

—WILLIE MAYS

Willie Mays can help a team just by riding on the bus with them.

—CHARLIE GRIMM, Cubs manager

I don't compare them, I just catch them.

—WILLIE MAYS, asked which of his catches he thought was the best

Willie Mays and his glove: where triples go to die.

— FRESCO THOMPSON, Dodgers executive

Watching him this year, seeing him drift across a base and then sink into full speed, I noticed all at once how much he resembles a marvelous skier in midturn down some steep pitch of fast powder. Nobody like him.

— ROGER ANGELL

I'm not sure I know just what the hell charisma is, but I get the feeling it's Willie Mays.

— TED KLUSZEWSKI, Reds first baseman

Willie Mays makes The Catch off a drive by Cleveland's Vic Wertz in the 1954 World Series at the Polo Grounds. Then, wrote Arnold Hanno, Mays "whirled and threw, like some olden statue of a Greek javelin hurler. . . . What an astonishing throw. This was the throw of a giant, the throw of a howitzer made human."

They invented the All-Star Game for Willie Mays.

—TED WILLIAMS

It's kind of fun now and then to use the names of real people in my comic strip, Peanuts. *And after looking over about 25 years' accumulation of strips, I discovered that I used the name Willie Mays more than any other individual. I suppose it's because, to me, Willie Mays has always symbolized perfection.*

—CHARLES SCHULZ

I started thinking about playing ball when I found out who Willie Mays was. . . . He could go O for four and beat you.

—REGGIE JACKSON

PADRE PITCHER MIKE CORKINS (distraught over giving up Mays's six hundreth homer): *Why'd it have to be me?*

MANAGER PRESTON GOMEZ: *Son, there've been five hundred and ninety-nine before you.*

I look at the kids over here and the way they're playing and the way they're fighting for themselves, and that says one thing to me: "Willie, say goodbye to America."

—WILLIE MAYS, announcing his retirement
from baseball on a day in his honor in 1973 at
Shea Stadium

Only a handful of players, in all baseball history, have been as important to winning teams, and have been able to contribute as much to eventual victory . . . as Mickey Mantle. Willie, on the other hand, I can sum up very simply: he's the best baseball player I ever saw.

—LEONARD KOPPETT, sportswriter

BROOKLYN: THE TEAM, THE PLACE

It was Brooklyn against the world. They were not only complete fanatics, but they knew baseball like the fans of no other city. It was exciting to play there. It was a treat. I walked into that crummy, flyblown park as Brooklyn manager for nine years, and every time I entered, my pulse quickened and my spirits soared.

—LEO DUROCHER

79

The Brooklyn Dodgers of 1952: Billy Cox, Pee Wee Reese, Duke Snider, Jackie Robinson, Roy Campanella, Andy Pafko, Gil Hodges, Carl Furillo, Joe Black. "Outspoken, opinionated, bigoted, tolerant, black, white, open, passionate: in short, a fascinating mix of vigorous men"—Roger Kahn.

That borough of churches and bad ball clubs, many of which I had.

—CASEY STENGEL

Summer or winter or any season, Flatbush fanatics don't need no reason. Leave us root for the Dodgers, Rodgers. That's the team for me.

—DAN PARKER, sportswriter

His swing is perfect, and this young man doesn't run on mere legs. Why, under him are two steel springs.

—BRANCH RICKEY, on Dodgers center fielder Duke Snider

Erv Palica had so many pitches, the catcher had to take off his mitt to give the sign.

—JOE BECKER

I got three pitches: my change; my change off my change; and my change off my change off my change.

—PREACHER ROE

That ain't a third baseman. That's a fucking acrobat.

—CASEY STENGEL, on fielding sensation Billy Cox

Every night when I go to bed I pray to the Lord and thank him for giving me the ability to play ball.

> —ROY CAMPANELLA, Dodgers catcher

I lost it in the sun.

> —BILLY LOES, Dodgers right-hander, on why
> he flubbed a ground ball

BRANCH RICKEY (after a bargaining session with Loes): *Billy, I'd appreciate it if you'd keep the terms of this contract secret.*
BILLY LOES: *Don't worry, I'm just as ashamed of the figures as you are.*

Just hold them for a few innings, fellas. I'll think of something.

> —CHARLIE DRESSEN, addressing the Dodgers
> late in a game

There were three million people in Brooklyn, and if every one of them wasn't rooting for the Dodgers, every one seemed to be.

> —RED BARBER

In Brooklyn, we had such great pennant races, it made the World Series just something that came later.

> —WALTER O'MALLEY, Dodgers owner

When I was a kid, there was nothing else. . . . We had Robinson, Reese and Furillo. We had Stanky and Hodges and Billy Cox. They came to us in the spring, as certain as rain and birds. They came on the radio, with Red Barber telling their tale, and there was nothing else we wanted.

> —PETE HAMILL

BALL PARK CHATTER

The greatest thrill in the world is to end the game with a home run and watch everybody else walk off the field while you're running the bases on air.

> —AL ROSEN, Indians third baseman

81

Many critics were surprised to know that the Browns could be bought because they didn't know the Browns were owned.

> —JOHN LARDNER, on the 1951 purchase of the
> St. Louis club by Bill Veeck

You'll never be a big winner until you start hating the hitter. That guy with the bat is trying to take your bread and butter away from you. You've got to fight him every second.

> —EARLY WYNN, Cleveland right-hander

I don't want to get to know the other guys too well. I might like them, and then I might not want to throw at them.

> —SAL "THE BARBER" MAGLIE, Giants right-
> hander

That space between the white lines—that's my office. That's where I conduct my business.

> —EARLY WYNN

I don't like losing a ball game any more than a salesman likes losing a sale. I've got a right to knock down anybody holding a bat.

> —EARLY WYNN. Once asked if he'd throw at
> his grandmother, Wynn replied, "Only if she
> was crowding the plate."

I try not to break the rules but merely to test their elasticity.

> —BILL VEECK

The Giants is dead.

> —CHARLIE DRESSEN, August 1951. The
> Dodgers manager's assessment was premature,
> however, for the Giants rallied from thirteen
> and one-half games down to tie the Dodgers in
> the regular season, then win the pennant in the
> third game of the play-offs on Bobby
> Thomson's ninth inning home run.

Now it is done. Now the story ends. And there is no way to tell it. The art of fiction is dead. Reality has strangled invention. Only the utterly impossible, the inexpressibly fantastic, can ever be plausible again.

> —RED SMITH, New York *Herald-Tribune*,
> reporting Thomson's historic blast

I never have much confidence in a pinch hitter, no matter who he is.

—JIMMY CANNON

They say I have to get to know my players. That arithmetic is bad. Isn't it simpler for twenty-five of them to get to know me?

—BIRDIE TEBBETTS, Reds manager

It proves that no man can be a success in two national pastimes.

—OSCAR LEVANT, on the break-up of Joe DiMaggio and Marilyn Monroe's marriage

Rabbit Maranville was working with kids for the Journal-American *when he died in January of 'fifty-four. The next summer he was voted into the Hall of Fame. Why did his record get so much better after he died?*

—JOHNNY MIZE

How did I feel when I heard the news [of his election to the Hall of Fame]? About the same way, I guess, that Columbus felt when he looked out from his ship and first saw land.

—DAZZY VANCE (1955)

Bobby Thomson is mobbed at the plate by his Giants teammates after hitting the miraculous home run that won the 1951 play-off. "The Giants win the pennant! The Giants win the pennant! I don't believe it—the Giants win the pennant"—Russ Hodges, broadcasting over radio.

Robin Roberts gave up an all-time record of forty-six home runs in 1956. "In the long history of organized baseball I stand unparalleled for putting Christianity into practice," he wrote. "And to prove I was not prejudiced, I served up home run balls to Negroes, Italians, Jews, Catholics alike. Race, creed, nationality made no difference to me."

Hitting is timing. Pitching is upsetting timing.

—Warren Spahn

I make my living off the hungriness of the hitter.

—Lew Burdette, Braves right-hander

If Lew could cook, I'd marry him.

—Fred Haney, Braves manager, after Burdette won three complete games in the '57 Series

I came to the Braves on business, and I intended to see that business was good as long as I could.

—Henry Aaron

Throwing a fastball by Henry Aaron is like trying to sneak the sunrise past a rooster.

—Curt Simmons, Phillies left-hander

I didn't get all the publicity that some of the other players got. . . . So eventually I decided, well, I'm going to go for the home run.

—Henry Aaron

Reporter: *What's the key to hitting for a high average?*
Stan Musial: *Relax, concentrate—and don't hit the fly ball to center field.*

Without him, the Cubs would finish in Albuquerque.

—Jimmy Dykes, rival manager, on Ernie Banks

Ernie Banks leaps to snag an errant throw in a 1954 game against the Giants. It's safe to say Mike Royko was not referring to Mr. Cub when he wrote, "As a lifetime Cubs fan, I was used to players who, as the sportswriters say, 'can do it all.' In the case of the Cubs, 'doing it all' means striking out, running the wrong way, falling down, dropping the ball."

Who needs New York?

> —WARREN GILES, president of the National League, when asked if he thought the League would suffer when the Giants and Dodgers moved West in 1958

REPORTER: *How do you feel about the kids in New York from whom you are taking the Giants?*

GIANTS OWNER HORACE STONEHAM: *I feel bad about the kids, but I haven't seen many of their fathers lately.*

This ball. This symbol. Is it worth a man's life?

> —BRANCH RICKEY

DYNASTY (PART II)

Rooting for the New York Yankees is like rooting for U. S. Steel.

—RED SMITH (1951)

There is no such thing as second place. Either you're first or you're nothing.

—GEORGE WEISS, Yankees executive

I never have been on a yacht in my whole life. But I imagine rooting for the Yankees is like owning a yacht.

—JIMMY CANNON. Another time Cannon wrote,
"The Giants were our team. We left the
tourists to the Yankees."

I'll tell you what I think of our prospects. I think we've got the world by the ears, and we're not letting go.

—CASEY STENGEL, Yankees manager

When you're walking to the bank with that World Series check every November, you don't want to leave. There were no Yankees saying play me or trade me.

—HANK BAUER, Yankees outfielder

Johnny Sain don't say much, but that don't matter much, because when you're out there on the mound, you got nobody to talk to.

—CASEY STENGEL

I never blame myself when I'm not hitting. I just blame the bat and if it keeps up I change bats. . . . After all, if I know it isn't my fault that I'm not hitting, how can I get mad at myself?

—YOGI BERRA

So I'm ugly. So what? I never saw anyone hit with his face.

—YOGI BERRA

He was a peculiar fellow with amazing ability.

—CASEY STENGEL, on Yogi Berra

My best pitch is anything the batter grounds, lines or pops in the direction of [Phil] Rizzuto.

—VIC RASCHI, Yankees right-hander

If I were a retired gentleman, I would follow the Yankees around just to see Rizzuto work those miracles every day.

—CASEY STENGEL

Bobby Brown reminds me of a fellow who's been hitting for twelve years and fielding one.

—CASEY STENGEL

He played first base and the outfield, pinch hit, and did everything but collect tickets.

—CASEY STENGEL, on Tommy Byrne

REPORTER (in the clubhouse after Don Larsen's 1956 World Series perfect game): *Casey, was this the best game you ever saw Larsen pitch?*
CASEY STENGEL: *So far.*

Jerry Lumpe looks like the best hitter in the world until you put him in the lineup.

—CASEY STENGEL

It's easy to have a good day when you feel good, and easy to have a horseshit day when you feel horseshit. The question is, when you feel horseshit, can you still have a good day?

—GIL MCDOUGALD, Yankees infielder

I would not admire hitting against [Ryne] Duren, because if he ever hit you in the head you might be in the past tense.

—CASEY STENGEL

You would be amazed how many important outs you can get by working the count down to where the hitter is sure you're going to throw to his weakness and then throw to his power instead.

—WHITEY FORD

"That Mantle ever played again after his first knee operation is testimony to his personal drive to perform; that he continued to play hurt for seventeen more years became part of his legend"–Peter Gent.

He was my banty rooster. Whitey used to stick out his chest, like this, and walk out on the mound against any of those big pitchers. They talk about the fall of the Yankees. Well, the Yankees would have fallen a lot sooner if it wasn't for my banty rooster.

—CASEY STENGEL

I don't like to be made a big thing of. I just like to go someplace, and you buy one and I buy one.

—WHITEY FORD

Look at Bobby Richardson. He doesn't drink, he doesn't smoke, and he still can't hit .250.

—CASEY STENGEL

It was all I lived for, to play ball.

—MICKEY MANTLE

I don't quite know how to put it. What I'm trying to tell you is that the first time I saw Mantle, I knew how Paul Krichell felt when he first saw Lou Gehrig. He knew that as a scout he'd never have another moment like it. I felt the same way about Mantle.

—TOM GREENWADE, the scout who discovered
the Yankee center fielder

I wish I was half the ballplayer he is.

—AL KALINE, on Mantle

All I have is natural ability.

—MICKEY MANTLE

Mantle had it in his body to be great.

—CASEY STENGEL

I always loved the game, but when my legs weren't hurting, it was a lot easier to love.

—MICKEY MANTLE

I've often wondered how a man who knew he was going to die could stand here and say he was the luckiest man on the face of the earth, but now I guess I know how he felt.

—MICKEY MANTLE, on "Mickey Mantle Day"
at Yankee Stadium, June 1969

7
STENGELESE SPOKEN HERE

○ FOR THOSE not familiar with the life and legend of Casey Stengel, a brief explanation may be in order. Casey played and managed baseball for more than half a century. His greatest managerial success came with the Yankees when he guided them to ten pennants and seven World Championships in twelve seasons. Then, in 1962, in an amazing turnabout, he became the first manager of the New York Mets, one of the worst teams in baseball history. Oh yes, one other thing about Casey: he talked funny.

The secret of managing a club is to keep the five guys who hate you away from the five who are undecided.

—CASEY STENGEL

Ability is the art of getting credit for all the home runs somebody else hits.

—CASEY STENGEL

All right, everyone, line up alphabetically according to your height.

—CASEY, instructing his players in spring training

Casey at the bat in 1922. Sizing up the young Casey, a scout said, "He's a dandy ballplayer except for one thing: it's from his shoulders down."

He can talk all day and all night, and on any kind of track, wet or dry.

> —JOHN LARDNER, on Casey

Wake up, muscles! We're in New York now.

> —YOUNG CASEY STENGEL, arriving at the Polo Grounds in 1921 to play for the Giants

I mighta been able to make it as a pitcher except for one thing. I had a rather awkward motion and every time I brought my left arm forward I hit myself in the ear.

> —CASEY, reminiscing about his playing days

I was such a dangerous hitter I even got intentional walks in batting practice.

> —CASEY

Well, Casey Stengel just can't help being Casey Stengel.

> —KENESAW MOUNTAIN LANDIS, asked why he hadn't fined Stengel more for acting up during a World Series game in 1923

I don't play cards, I don't play golf, and I don't go to the picture show. All that is left is baseball.

> —CASEY STENGEL

Nice to meet ya, King.

> —CASEY, greeting George V of England during a 1924 barnstorming tour

It used to be that you had to catch the ball two-handed because the glove was so small. Why, when I got married I couldn't afford dress gloves, so I wore my baseball mitt to my wedding and nobody even noticed. That took care of my right hand, and I was smart enough to keep my left hand in my pocket.

> —CASEY STENGEL

Edna, my wife, is good with money. When Edna was a girl, she worked in a movie house for two dollars and fifty cents. She still has that same two dollars and fifty cents.

> —CASEY STENGEL

Edna Lawson, best catch I ever made.

—CASEY STENGEL

Left-handers have more enthusiasm for life. They sleep on the wrong side of the bed and their head gets more stagnant on that side.

—CASEY STENGEL

People ask me, "Casey, how can you speak so much when you don't talk English too good?" Well, I've been invited to Europe, and I say, "They don't speak English over there too good, either."

—CASEY STENGEL

It ain't sex that's troublesome, it's staying up all night looking for it.

—CASEY STENGEL

You gotta learn that if you don't get it by midnight, chances are you ain't gonna get it, and if you do, it ain't worth it.

—CASEY, on the same subject

This is a big job, fellows, and I barely have had time to study it. In fact, I scarcely know where I am at.

—CASEY, at the 1948 press conference
announcing his appointment as Yankee
manager

I couldna done it without my players.

—CASEY, accepting congratulations for another
Yankee pennant

What I learned from McGraw I used with all of them. They're still playing with a round ball, a round bat, and nine guys on a side.

—CASEY STENGEL

What's the use of askin' a man to execute if he can't execute?

—CASEY STENGEL

When we are getting some hits we aren't getting them when we have somebody on the bases. It's very aggravating. But maybe it's better to see them left there than not getting them on at all. If they keep getting on you got to figure one of these days they'll be getting home. Or it could be one of these years, you know.

—CASEY STENGEL

It's like I used to tell my barber. Shave and a haircut but don't cut my throat. I may want to do that myself.

—CASEY STENGEL

See that fella over there? He's twenty years old. In ten years he's got a chance to be a star. Now that other fella over there, he's twenty years old, too. In ten years he's got a chance to be thirty.

—CASEY STENGEL

They say some of my stars drink whiskey, but I have found that the ones who drink milkshakes don't win many ball games.

—CASEY STENGEL

REPORTER: *What's the secret to platooning?*

CASEY: *There's not much to it. You put a right-hand hitter against a left-hand pitcher and a left-hand hitter against a right-hand pitcher and on cloudy days you use a fastball pitcher.*

A double play gives you two twenty-sevenths of a ball game.

—CASEY STENGEL

I had many years that I was not successful as a ballplayer, as it is a game of skill. And then I was no doubt discharged by baseball in which I had to go back to the minor leagues as a manager, and after being in the minor leagues as a manager, I became a major

Before the Ol' Perfesser achieved success with the Yankees, traditionalists dismissed him as a flake. While managing the '43 Braves, Casey was hit by a cab and laid up for part of the season. One sarcastic writer nominated the cabbie as "the man who has done the most for Boston baseball."

Casey kept a cool head during his days as manager of the hapless Mets. "Without losers," he philosophized, "where would the winners be?"

league manager in several cities and was discharged. We call it discharged because there is no question I had to leave.

> —CASEY, testifying before a 1958 Senate subcommittee investigating baseball's exemption from antitrust laws. After a stream of vintage Stengelese left the senators completely baffled, Mickey Mantle was then asked to speak. "My views are just about the same as Casey's," he said.

I don't like them fellas who drive in two runs and let in three.

> —CASEY STENGEL

I always heard it couldn't be done, but sometimes it don't always work.

> —CASEY STENGEL

REPORTER: *The Associated Press has a bulletin, Casey. It says you were fired [by the Yankees]. What about it?*

CASEY STENGEL: *What do I care what the AP says. Their opinion ain't gonna send me into any fainting spell. Anyway, what about the UP?*

95

I'll never make the mistake of being seventy again.

—CASEY STENGEL, after he was discharged by
the Yankees in 1960 for being "too old"

I'll tell ya something. They examined all my organs. Some of them are quite remarkable, and others are not so good. A lot of museums are bidding on them.

—CASEY, after a hospital visit

Everybody keeps saying how good I'm looking. Well, maybe I do. But they should see me inside. I look terrible inside.

—CASEY STENGEL

It's great to be back in the Polar Grounds. It's a great honor for me to be joining the Knickerbockers.

—CASEY, on being named manager of the Mets
in 1962

You have to have a catcher, because if you don't, you're likely to have a lot of passed balls.

—CASEY STENGEL, on why the Mets chose a
catcher as their first pick in the expansion draft

Now there's three things you can do in a baseball game: you can win or you can lose or it can rain.

—CASEY STENGEL

Excuse me, Mr. President, but I hafta go to work.

—CASEY to John Kennedy, before the 1962 All-
Star Game

I stayed up last night and watched the Republican Convention all night long. I watched all of them talk, and listened to them and seen them and I'm not interested in politics. If you watch them and listen to them you can find out why you're not.

—CASEY STENGEL

You gotta lose 'em some time. When you do, lose 'em right.

—CASEY STENGEL

I'm probably the only guy who worked for Stengel before and after he became a genius.

> —WARREN SPAHN, who played for Casey in the early '40s when he managed the Braves and in his last year as manager of the Mets

Most ball games are lost, not won.

> —CASEY STENGEL

I love signing autographs. I'll sign anything but veal cutlets. My ball point pen slips on veal cutlets.

> —CASEY STENGEL

Oldtimers weekends and airplane landings are alike. If you can walk away from them, they're successful.

> —CASEY STENGEL

Most people my age are dead at the present time, and you could look it up.

> —CASEY STENGEL, age seventy-five

Just because your legs is dead don't mean your head is.

> —CASEY STENGEL

I want to thank my parents for letting me play baseball, and I'm thankful I had baseball knuckles and couldn't become a dentist.

> —CASEY, at his induction into the Hall of Fame in 1966

I chased the balls that Babe Ruth hit.

> —CASEY, reminiscing about his career at the induction ceremonies

When I played in Brooklyn, I could go to the ball park for a nickel carfare. But now I live in Pasadena, and it costs me fifteen or sixteen dollars to take a cab to Glendale. If I was a young man, I'd study to become a cabdriver.

> —CASEY STENGEL

REPORTER: *Would you like to go back to managing?*

CASEY STENGEL: *Well, to be perfectly truthful and honest and frank about it, I am eighty-five years old, which ain't bad, so to be truthful and honest and frank about it, the thing I'd like to be right now is . . . an astronaut!*

Well, God is certainly getting an earful tonight.

—JIM MURRAY, sportswriter, on the death of
Casey Stengel, September 29, 1975

There comes a time in every man's life and I've had plenty of them.

—CASEY STENGEL

8
CHANGING TIMES: THE '60s

O CHANGE COMES slowly, and grudgingly, to baseball. What we now consider commonplace—the home run, night baseball, radio broadcasts—were once seen as threats to the game's integrity. So too did many traditionalists frown on the developments of this era: expansion, Astroturf, the rising influence of television, players' rights struggles. That baseball survived, indeed flourished, amidst this wave of change illustrates once again its remarkable resiliency.

THOSE AMAZIN' METS

We are a fraud.

—CASEY STENGEL, manager

From the start, the trouble with the Mets was the fact they were not too good at playing baseball. They lost an awful lot of games by one run, which is the mark of a bad team. They also lost innumerable games by fourteen runs or so. This is the mark of a terrible team. Actually, all the Mets did was lose. They lost at home and they lost away, they lost at night and they lost in the daytime. And they lost with maneuvers that shake the imagination.

—JIMMY BRESLIN

99

Our first Mets game was April 10, 1962. And it was our best game. It was rained out.

> —CASEY STENGEL

The only thing worse than a Mets game is a Mets doubleheader.

> —CASEY STENGEL

RAY DAVIAULT (after serving up a home run ball): *It was bad luck. I threw him a perfect pitch.*

CASEY STENGEL: *It couldn't have been a perfect pitch. Perfect pitches don't travel that far.*

The Mets is a very good thing. They give everybody a job. Just like the WPA.

> —BILLY LOES

The Mets have shown me ways to lose I never knew existed.

> —CASEY STENGEL

It stands to reason if the Yankees win one hundred games and lose sixty-two, the Yankee fan has endured sixty-two disappointments. If the Mets win fifty and lose one hundred twelve, the Met fan has had fifty thrills.

> —Anonymous sportswriter

Cranberry, Strawberry, We Love Throneberry!

> —Mets fans, chanting for error-prone first
> baseman "Marvelous" Marv Throneberry

Having Marv Throneberry play for your team is like having Willie Sutton play for your bank.

> —JIMMY BRESLIN

Look at that guy. He can't hit, he can't run, and he can't throw. Of course, that's why they gave him to us.

> --CASEY STENGEL

Some day I'll write a book and call it How I Got the Nickname "Pumpsie" *and sell it for one dollar, and if everybody who ever asked me that question buys the book, I'll be a millionaire.*

> —PUMPSIE GREEN, third baseman

The Mets led by Casey Stengel were loved by millions, despite losing more than one hundred games in each of their first three seasons. One fan's sign summed it up: "To Error Is Human, To Forgive Is a Met Fan."

We are in such a slump that even the ones that are drinkin' aren't hittin'.

—CASEY STENGEL

He wanted to see poverty, so he came to see my team.

—CASEY STENGEL, on a visit by President
Lyndon Johnson to Shea Stadium

The way some of my boys have been playing, I'd be better off if they were hurtin'.

—CASEY STENGEL

There is more Met than Yankee in every one of us.

—ROGER ANGELL

I don't know what's going on, but I know I've never seen it before.

—RICHIE ASHBURN, who finished his long,
distinguished career with the hapless Mets

You look up and down the bench and you have to say to yourself: "Can't anybody here play this game?"

—CASEY STENGEL

101

Sandy Koufax led the National League in ERA five years in a row and struck out 382 batters in 1965. "Sandy's fastball was so fast, some batters would start to swing as he was on his way to the mound" —Jim Murray.

DODGER BLUEBLOODS

You might say that the Dodgers were afraid to do anything wrong. This was fear at its finest.

—JOHN CARMICHAEL, after Los Angeles swept the Yankees in the 1963 Series

I became a good pitcher when I stopped trying to make them miss the ball and started trying to make them hit it.

—SANDY KOUFAX

Pitching is the art of instilling fear by making a man flinch.

—SANDY KOUFAX

It is almost painful to watch, for Koufax, instead of merely overpowering hitters, as some fastball throwers do, appears to dismantle them, taking away first one and then another of their carefully developed offensive weapons and judgments, and leaving them only with the conviction that they are the victims of a total mismatch.

—ROGER ANGELL

I can see how he won twenty-five games [this season]. What I don't understand is how he lost five.

— YOGI BERRA, after facing Koufax in the '63 Series

It is better to throw a theoretically poorer pitch wholeheartedly than to throw the so-called right pitch with a feeling of doubt. . . . You've got to feel sure you're doing the right thing—sure that you want to throw the pitch that you're going to throw.

— SANDY KOUFAX

I've got one way to pitch to righties—tight.

— DON DRYSDALE

If one of our guys went down, I just doubled it. No confusion there. It didn't require a Rhodes Scholar. If two of my teammates went down, four of yours would. I had to protect my guys.

— DON DRYSDALE

Don's idea of a waste pitch is a strike.

— JIM BROSNAN

I never hit anybody in the head on purpose. I aimed for their back. Or their ass.

— DON DRYSDALE

The trick against Drysdale is to hit him before he hits you.

— ORLANDO CEPEDA, Giants first baseman

Watching Frank Howard come out of the Dodger dugout to start a game is like watching the opening scene of a horror movie. You know the bit: there's an explosion under a polar ice cap some place, the earth rumbles and opens up, and out of it comes this Thing.

— JIM MURRAY

Frank Howard is so big, he wasn't born, he was founded.

— JIM MURRAY

I had a problem with money. I couldn't hold onto any.

— WILLIE DAVIS, Dodgers center fielder

103

It's not my life, it's not my wife, so why worry?

—WILLIE DAVIS, on why he never got rattled in pressure games

You know [Dodger manager] Walter Alston. The only guy in the game who could look Billy Graham right in the face without blushing [and] who would order corn on the cob in a Paris restaurant.

—JIM MURRAY

At third it's "be safe." That's because on a squeeze play it's better to leave too late than early. At second base I concentrate on one thing: "be careful." I'm already in scoring position, and it doesn't make sense to take chances. At first it's "be daring."

—MAURY WILLS

Once I get on first I become a pitcher and catcher as well as a base runner. I am trying to think with them.

—MAURY WILLS

If you get picked off or thrown out, you have to go right back and challenge the pitcher. It's like getting thrown off a horse; you have to get right back on.

—MAURY WILLS

There's no such thing as an unimportant stolen base.

—MAURY WILLS

BALL PARK CHATTER

Good pitching will beat good hitting any time, and vice versa.

—BOB VEALE, Pirates right-hander

If you don't play to win, why keep score?

—VERNON LAW, Pirates pitcher

Rocky Colavito will play left field for the Tigers, and he has the feet for it.

—JOE FALLS

Maury Wills steals his one hundred and fourth base of the
1962 season, then the most ever for a single year. Reds'
manager Fred Hutchinson said, "My instructions for
preventing Wills from stealing are simple. Don't let him
get on base."

We made too many wrong mistakes.

> —YOGI BERRA, on why the Yankees lost the
> 1960 World Series to the Pirates

Drinking is not a spectator sport.

> —JIM BROSNAN, Reds right-hander

*I don't want to be Babe Ruth. He was a great ballplayer. I'm not
trying to replace him. The record is there and damn right I want to
break it, but that isn't replacing Babe Ruth.*

> —ROGER MARIS (1961)

*The community of baseball feels Mantle is a great player. They
consider Maris a thrilling freak who batted .269.*

> —JIMMY CANNON

*Look at this. My goddam hair is coming out. Did your hair ever
fall out from playing baseball?*

> —ROGER MARIS

105

It would have been a helluva lot more fun if I had never hit those sixty-one home runs. . . . All it brought me was headaches.

—ROGER MARIS

When I'm pitching I feel I'm down to the essentials. Two men, with one challenge between them, and what better challenge than between pitcher and hitter?

—WARREN SPAHN

I just won the Nobel Prize of baseball.

—ELSTON HOWARD, after hearing he'd received the 1963 AL Most Valuable Player award

My only regret in life is that I can't sit in the stands and watch me pitch.

—BO BELINSKY. After throwing a no-hitter in 1962, the Angels' glamour boy said, "If I'd known I was gonna pitch a no-hitter today, I would have gotten a haircut."

I need her like Custer needed Indians.

—BO BELINSKY, on why he was splitting up with actress Mamie Van Doren

Baseball makes broads aggressive.

—JIM BROSNAN

Almost every batter guesses a few times in a game. This is an advantage for me. . . . Hell, most of the time I don't know what I'm going to throw.

—SAM MCDOWELL, Indians pitcher

Any pitcher who throws at a batter and deliberately tries to hit him is a Communist.

—ALVIN DARK, Giants manager

Dark throws stools. Hutch throws rooms.

—ED BAILEY, on the contrasting managerial styles of Al Dark and Fred Hutchinson

At age forty-two Warren Spahn won twenty-three games and lost seven for Milwaukee. Stan Musial said, "I don't think Spahn will ever get into the Hall of Fame. He'll never stop pitching."

Where is the magic that was Mantle?
Kubek to Moose, a double play.
I don't recall growing older.
When did they?
> —JERRY IZENBERG, sportswriter, on the demise of the Yankees dynasty

Stu Miller has three speeds—slow, slower and slowest.
> —Anonymous

Stan Musial at the end of his career. "Here stands baseball's perfect warrior. Here stands baseball's perfect knight"—Ford Frick.

To hit Stu Miller a batter needs the patience of a guy waiting for his wife to get dressed to go out. . . . Around the league, they are waiting for the day some eager rookie gets two swings at the same pitch.

—JIM MURRAY

Bob Gibson is the luckiest pitcher I ever saw. He always pitches when the other team doesn't score any runs.

—TIM MCCARVER, Cardinals catcher

Gibson pitches as though he's double-parked.

—VIN SCULLY

I never considered taking him out. I had a commitment to his heart.

—JOHNNY KEANE, Cardinals manager, on why
he refused to pull a struggling Bob Gibson late
in the seventh game of the 1964 World Series

REPORTER: *How much difference does a manager make?*
BILL WHITE: *It depends on the manager.*

My God, they've hired the Unknown Soldier.

—LARRY FOX, sportswriter, on hearing that a
retired Air Force general, William Eckert, had
been named commissioner of baseball

LON SIMMONS (conducting a postgame interview): *Gee, Jim, you really looked hungry out on the field.*

GIANTS THIRD BASEMAN JIM RAY HART: *That's right, Lon. I hadn't eaten breakfast yet.*

I'd yank my own son if it was the right move.
> —EDDIE STANKY, White Sox manager (Once after a bad White Sox loss the fiery Stanky barred the clubhouse to all visitors. When told that Vice President Hubert Humphrey wanted to see the players, Stanky said, "What do we need him for? He can't hit.")

Bench me or trade me.
> —GEORGE THOMAS, Red Sox outfielder

Umpires are most vigorous when defending their miscalls.
> —JIM BROSNAN

Juan Marichal. "If you placed all the pitchers in the history of the game behind a transparent curtain, where only a silhouette was visible, Juan's motion would be the easiest to identify. He brought to the mound . . . beauty, individuality and class"—Bob Stevens.

WILLIE HORTON: *I got a good education in high school. I took all kinds of good courses. What did you take in high school, Gates?*

GATES BROWN: *I took a little English, a little math, some science, a few hubcaps and some wheel covers.*

Spring is a time of year when the ground thaws, trees bud, the income tax falls due—and everybody wins the pennant.
>   —JIM MURRAY

One thing I can tell you. This is not an eighth-place team.
>   —LEO DUROCHER, addressing the press after
>   being named Cubs manager in 1966. The Cubs
>   finished tenth that season.

Luis Tiant comes from everywhere except between his legs.
>   —CURT GOWDY

Oakland is the luckiest city since Hiroshima.
>   —SENATOR STUART SYMINGTON of Missouri, on
>   hearing that Charlie Finley had moved the A's
>   to Oakland from Kansas City

Show me a guy who's afraid to look bad and I'll show you a guy you can beat every time.
>   —LOU BROCK

I don't have to steal bases, you see, to play. I steal bases because I want to.
>   —LOU BROCK

To a pitcher a base hit is the perfect example of negative feedback.
>   —STEVE HOVLEY, Pilots outfielder

Don't forget to swing hard, in case you hit the ball.
>   —WOODIE HELD, journeyman infielder

My God, they've elected a race track.
>   —A critic, on hearing that Bowie Kuhn had
>   been elected commissioner

110

Brooks Robinson is not a fast man, but his arms and legs move very quickly.

—Curt Gowdy

I could field as long as I can remember. But hitting has been a struggle all my life.

—Brooks Robinson

He plays third like he was sent down from another league.

—Ed Hurley, on Brooks Robinson

If Boog Powell held out his right arm, he'd be a railroad crossing.

—Joe Garagiola

Carl Yastrzemski terrorized American League opponents in 1967 when he won batting's triple crown. Said Yankees catcher Elston Howard, "We try everything on Yaz and nothing works. The only thing you can do against him is pitch him tight . . . and hope."

Tom Seaver (top) won twenty-five games and Jerry Koosman (bottom) seventeen to lead the Miracle Mets to the 1969 pennant. After the Mets beat the Orioles in five games to win the World Championship, a delighted Casey Stengel said, "Well, they're still my boys, ain't they?"

Frank was not out to make friends but to knock someone on his tail.

> —BROOKS ROBINSON, on Orioles teammate
> Frank Robinson

You don't always make an out. Sometimes the pitcher gets you out.

> —CARL YASTRZEMSKI

REPORTER: *Would you rather face Jim Palmer or Tom Seaver?*
MERV RETTENMUND: *That's like asking if I'd rather be hung or go to the electric chair.*

A good professional athlete must have the love of a little boy. And the good players feel the kind of love for the game that they did when they were Little Leaguers.

> —TOM SEAVER

That classic duel between pitcher and batter is fascinating. No other sport has such a dramatic and vivid confrontation. I live my life around the four days between starts.

> —TOM SEAVER

So many of the owners think of me and all the other players essentially as laborers. They have no appreciation of the artistic value of what I do. . . . How can they be in baseball and not see what it's all about? Pitching is a beautiful thing. It's an art.

> —TOM SEAVER

We are here to prove there is no Santa Claus.

> —BROOKS ROBINSON, before the Orioles met
> the upstart Mets in the '69 Series

This is the first time. Nothing can ever be as sweet again.

> —RON SWOBODA, after the Mets whipped the
> Orioles to win their first World Championship

9
NEW LIFE IN THE OLD GAME: THE SEVENTIES

○ BASEBALL WAS plagued by controversy and self-doubt during the '60s and early '70s, but on a New England night in 1975 all its troubles were forgotten. Just as Bobby Thomson's epochal blast twenty-four years earlier had moved the entire nation, almost every baseball fan can tell you where they were and what they were doing when Carlton Fisk hit a fly ball against the left field foul pole of Fenway Park for a home run to win the sixth game of that marvelous World Series. That magic, incandescent moment signaled the start of a new baseball revival, propelling it into an undreamt age of fan interest, glory and big money.

CHARLIE O. AND THE FEUDING A'S

We had a common bond on the A's: everybody hated Charlie Finley.
— REGGIE JACKSON

My middle initial stands for Owner.
                    —CHARLIE O. FINLEY

If a manager of mine ever said someone was indispensable, I'd fire him.
                    —CHARLIE FINLEY

He has been wonderful to me. I have nothing but the highest regard for him.
                    —DICK WILLIAMS, A's manager, on Charlie
                    Finley (1973)

A man can take just so much of Finley.
                    —DICK WILLIAMS (1974)

Anyone can manage a baseball team. The owner runs the team anyway.
                    —CHARLIE FINLEY

Finley is so cold-blooded, he ought to make antifreeze commercials.
                    —REGGIE JACKSON

Prospects are a dime a dozen.
                    —CHARLIE FINLEY

As Reggie Jackson led the A's to three world titles in the early '70s, his reputation became firmly established. Dock Ellis called him "the chocolate hot dog." A's teammate Darrold Knowles added, "There isn't enough mustard in the world to cover Reggie Jackson."

It's a weird scene. You win a few baseball games and all of a sudden you're surrounded by reporters and TV men with cameras asking you about Vietnam and race relations.

—VIDA BLUE (1971)

Everyone wants my time, and I don't have any time left. I'm a person, not a headline.

—VIDA BLUE

I think I have signed some scrap of paper for every man, woman and child in the United States.

—VIDA BLUE

Nothing mysterious about [Catfish] Hunter. He just throws strikes.

—EARL WEAVER. After giving up two home runs to the Dodgers in a 1974 World Series game, Hunter explained, "I had some friends here from North Carolina, and they'd never seen a home run, so I gave 'em a couple."

What they start, I finish.

—ROLLIE FINGERS

Sweat plus sacrifice equals success.

—CHARLIE FINLEY's motto. Much to the A's distress, "S + S = S" was engraved on their 1973 championship rings.

I'm going to write a book about my days with Finley. I'm going to call it, And They Thought I Was Crazy.

—JIMMY PIERSALL

Finley is a self-made man who worships his creator.

—JIM MURRAY

I have often called Bowie Kuhn the village idiot. I apologize to all the village idiots of America. He's the nation's idiot.

—CHARLIE FINLEY

A woman asked me the other day if there's any truth to the rumor that Charlie Finley is out to get me. I said, "Honey, that ain't no rumor."

—BOWIE KUHN

Charlie Finley wouldn't think God would make a good commissioner.
> —WARREN GILES

Sometimes I even amaze myself.
> —REGGIE JACKSON

There was only one big home run guy, one big hero. That was Reggie. He was born to the job.
> —DAVE DUNCAN, teammate on the A's

If I played in New York, they'd name a candy bar after me.
> —REGGIE JACKSON

The thing about Reggie is that you know he's going to produce. And if he doesn't, he's going to talk enough to make people think he's going to produce.
> —CATFISH HUNTER

With me, everybody in the ball park knows I'll be running, so I'm not stealing anything. I'm taking something. I am a basetaker.
> —BILL NORTH, A's center fielder

They're going to retire my uniform . . . with me still in it.
> —BILLY CONIGLIARO, A's bench-warmer

Was it difficult leaving the Titanic?
> —SAL BANDO, asked if it was hard to leave the Finley-owned A's

BALL PARK CHATTER

The only thing running and exercising can do for you is make you healthy.
> —MICKEY LOLICH, portly Tigers left-hander

When you're hitting the ball, it comes at you looking like a grapefruit. When you're not, it looks like a black-eyed pea.
> —GEORGE SCOTT, Red Sox slugger

117

Roberto Clemente led the Pirates to their 1971 World
Championship and demonstrated, as Roger Angell wrote, "a
kind of baseball that none of us had ever seen before—throwing
and running and hitting at something close to the level of
absolute perfection."

*When I am right, no one remembers. When I am wrong, no one
forgets.*

      —DOUG HARVEY, umpire

*I'm not sure which is more insulting, being offered in a trade or
having it turned down.*

      —CLAUDE OSTEEN, Dodgers southpaw

I am a man, not a consignment of goods to be bought and sold.

      —CURT FLOOD, explaining why he filed suit
      against the reserve clause in early 1970

"How you play the game" is for college boys. When you're play-ing for money, winning is the only thing that counts.

—LEO DUROCHER

Win any way you can as long as you can get away with it.

—LEO DUROCHER

I consider myself one of the best players baseball has had. I won't say the best because there have been some great ones.

—HENRY AARON

I'd rather play in Hell than for the Angels.

—ALEX JOHNSON, after being traded to California. He went on to win the 1970 AL batting title as an Angel.

I once called the president of Vaseline and told him he should use me in a commercial since I use his product all the time. He got a little upset when he found out what I use it for. He said Vaseline is for babies' fannies, not baseballs.

—GAYLORD PERRY

There's no place in the game for what Gaylord Perry does to a baseball. Baseball is a clean game.

—FELIPE ALOU, Perry's former teammate on the Giants

If you stand next to Perry, he smells like a drugstore.

—BILLY MARTIN

Some people give their bodies to science; I give mine to baseball.

—RON HUNT, who holds the major league career record for most times being hit by a pitched ball, 243

When I was a kid, I used to imagine animals running under my bed. I told my dad, and he solved the problem quickly. He cut the legs off the bed.

—LOU BROCK

REPORTER: *How do you feel now that the [1971] Giants have clinched the divisional title?*

GIANTS CATCHER DICK DIETZ: *I feel great—and the Dodgers can go to hell!*

Why am I wasting so much dedication on a mediocre career?

    —RON SWOBODA

My best game plan is to sit on the bench and call out specific instructions like "C'mon Boog," "Get hold of one, Frank" or "Let's go, Brooks."

    —EARL WEAVER, on managing the 1971 Orioles

Instead of having my parents scream at me, now I have Earl Weaver.

    —JIM PALMER

All Earl [Weaver] knows about pitching is that he couldn't hit it.

    —MIKE CUELLAR, Orioles left-hander

You spend a good piece of your life gripping a baseball and in the end it turns out that it was the other way around all the time.

    —JIM BOUTON

Money is not the issue. The real issue is the owners' attempt to punish the players for having the audacity not to crawl.

    —MARVIN MILLER, executive director of the players' association, on the 1972 players' strike

Marvin Miller has struck out. He would do the game of baseball a great favor if he disappeared, got lost or found the nearest hole and jumped into it.

    —St. Louis *Globe-Democrat* (1972)

Brooks Robinson, said sportswriter Gordon Beard, "never asked anyone to name a candy bar after him. In Baltimore people name their children after him."

His bearing, his approach, his terminology belong on a soapbox around the corner from a struck factory. [Marvin] Miller's effect on the game has caused an alarming spiritual erosion.

> —FURMAN BISHER, sportswriter. Later, upset over the 1981 baseball strike, Dick Young would describe Miller as "the Merchant of Menace."

This strike was not for the Hank Aarons . . . or Willie Mayses. It was for the four-year players who pass up college, spend three to five years to make the majors, and have a career ruined by a dead arm or leg.

> —HOWARD COSELL (1972)

I want to say something personal to my father. Wake up, Dad, you just made it in.

> —JOSH GIBSON, JR., on the induction of his late father into the Hall of Fame in 1972

Statistics are about as interesting as first base coaches.

> —JIM BOUTON

Each club has a special hitting personality. One club will watch your delivery and say, "Oh boy, here comes a fastball," and they'll jump on it. Others say, "Oh boy, here's a change-up." The Pirates just say, "Oh boy, here comes a baseball."

> —DON SUTTON on the '73 Pirates

I never thought I'd see anything like this in America. But then, who says New York is America?

> —SPARKY ANDERSON, on the near-riot at Shea Stadium after the Mets clinched the pennant in 1973

I don't think those people at Wrigley Field ever saw but two players they liked. Billy Williams and Ernie Banks. Billy never said anything and Ernie always said the right thing.

> —FERGUSON JENKINS, who was traded to Texas in 1973 after eight seasons with the Cubs

If you ain't got a bull pen, you ain't got nuthin'.

> —YOGI BERRA

Henry Aaron hits number 715, breaking Babe Ruth's career home run mark. Said a relieved Aaron, perhaps reflecting on the media circus that chased him as he closed in on the record, "I just thank God it's all over."

REPORTER: *What makes a good manager?*
YOGI BERRA: *A good ball club.*

As a pitcher, I feel I'm creating something. Pitching itself is not enjoyable while you're doing it. Pitching is work. I don't enjoy it until I can stand back and look at what I've created. That is something.
                              —TOM SEAVER

Blind people come to the park just to listen to him pitch.
                              —REGGIE JACKSON, on Tom Seaver

REPORTER: *How does it feel to be the smallest player in the major leagues?*
FREDDIE PATEK: *It's better than being the smallest player in the minor leagues.*

The first look the Kansas City Royals got at Frederick Joseph Patek, they figured there must be a slow leak at Disneyland.
                              —JIM MURRAY

If you can cheat, I wouldn't wait one pitch longer.
                              —GEORGE BAMBERGER, Oriole coach, advising
                              left-hander Ross Grimsley in a jam

THE BIG RED MACHINE

This is some kind of game, isn't it?
                              —PETE ROSE to Carlton Fisk, in the tenth
                              inning of the sixth game of the 1975 Series

Most people don't understand catchers. For example, Jerry Grote is a catcher who hits. Johnny Bench is a hitter who catches. There is a big difference.
                              —JOE TORRE

There is a stillness about the Cincinnati Reds' Johnny Bench. It is the serenity of the hunter waiting in silence for the birds to fly down into range.
                              —JIMMY CANNON

Pete Rose in a customary pose. "I have never seen anyone come to the park with his enthusiasm, determination and desire. It's like every day is Opening Day"—Joe Morgan.

When I play the outfield or infield, it's almost like not playing at all. Catching is the most important job in baseball.

—JOHNNY BENCH

Every time Bench throws, everybody in baseball drools.

—HARRY DALTON, baseball executive

A moral victory to me is holding George Foster to a single.

—JOE SAMBITO, Astros reliever

There are four parts of self that lead to success. The first part is discipline, the second is concentration, third is patience, and fourth is faith.

—GEORGE FOSTER, Reds outfielder

Confidence is everything. Consider what the highest possible goal you can attain is and then convince yourself you can attain it.

—JOE MORGAN two-time NL MVP

I have more than average pride.

—PETE ROSE

I'm not a great runner. I'm no Joe Morgan, but I'm not bad for a white guy.

—PETE ROSE

He gets base hits in the present and lives in the past.

—LARRY MERCHANT, sportswriter, on Pete Rose

He's a ballplayer right off a Saturday Evening Post *cover. When you see Pete Rose coming down the street with a baseball bat, you look around to see if he's got his dog with him.*

—JIM MURRAY

Pete Rose is the greatest salesman baseball has.

—TOMMY LASORDA

Somebody's gotta win and somebody's gotta lose—and I believe in letting the other guy lose.

—PETE ROSE

The only way I can't hit .300 is if there is something physically wrong with me.

—PETE ROSE

Here lies the man who could hit forever.

—PETE ROSE, suggesting his epitaph

If anybody plays harder than Pete Rose, he's gotta be an outpatient.

—TUG McGRAW

Pete's not going to die of old age, he's going to die of prolonged boyhood.

—JIM MURRAY

I like to think of myself as a grownup playing like a kid.

—PETE ROSE

MORE CHATTER

Your body is just like a bar of soap. It gradually wears down from repeated use.

—DICK ALLEN, toward the end of his career

Watching a spring training game is as exciting as watching a tree form its annual ring.

—JERRY IZENBERG

I like my players to be married and in debt. That's the way you motivate them.

—ERNIE BANKS, coaching in the Cubs' minor league farm system

One thing about the Chicago Bears. When their season starts, it sure takes the heat off us Cubs.

—BILL MADLOCK, one-time Cubs third baseman

Fingers has 35 saves. Rollie has a better record than John the Baptist.

—LON SIMMONS, sportscaster

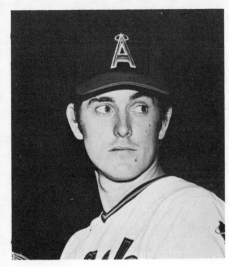

Nolan Ryan pitched four no-hitters in three seasons for the Angels on the strength of an overpowering fastball. Said Don Sutton, "His changeup is the same as my fastball."

Things were so bad in Chicago last summer that by the fifth inning we were selling hot dogs to go.

—KEN BRETT, recalling his 1976 season on the White Sox

If you're looking for job security, drive a mail truck. Managers always get fired.

—ALVIN DARK, former manager

I resent the charges that we intentionally blacked out the city to help save the Yankees. The blackout was an act of God, and even God couldn't save the Yankees.

—Con Edison spokesman, on the 1977 New York City blackout

I'm not interested in selling the Braves . . . but I don't know why not.

—TED TURNER, Braves owner

It took me seventeen years to get three thousand hits. I did it in one afternoon on the golf course.

—HENRY AARON

I am dead set against free agency. It can ruin baseball.

—GEORGE STEINBRENNER

As men get older, the toys get more expensive.

> —MARVIN DAVIS, explaining why he bid a
> rumored twelve million dollars to buy the A's

Trying to hit Phil Niekro is like trying to eat Jell-O with chopsticks. Sometimes you might get a piece, but most of the time you get hungry.

> —BOBBY MURCER

Baseball is the best sport for a writer to cover, because it's daily. It's ongoing. You have to fill the need, write the daily soap opera.

> —PETER GAMMONS, sportswriter

If I'd done everything I was supposed to, I'd be leading the league in homers, have the highest batting average, have given one hundred thousand dollars to the Cancer Fund, and be married to Marie Osmond.

> —CLINT HURDLE, Royals outfielder, on what it
> was like to be a young "phenom" breaking into
> the majors

Dave Parker, the National League's 1978 most valuable player, is not known for his shyness. "I'm wall to wall and tree-top tall," he told a reporter. "Two things's for sure, the sun's gonna shine and I'm going three for four."

This winter I'm working out every day, throwing at a wall. I'm eleven and 0 against the wall.

> —JIM BOUTON, making a comeback at age thirty-eight

I signed Oscar Gamble on the advice of my attorney. I no longer have Gamble and I no longer have my attorney.

> —RAY KROC, Padres owner

The minor leagues aren't really all that hard to take. You can sleep in and read the sports pages.

> —BOBBY DEWS, former minor league manager

They have positive momentum, while we have negative momentum.

> —BILL LEE, on why the Yankees were catching the Red Sox late in the '78 season

Jim Rice and I arrived in New England about the same time. Now he's got about five million, and I get to cover the Celtics.

> —LARRY WHITESIDE, sportswriter

If I ain't startin', I ain't departin'.

> —GARRY TEMPLETON, refusing to play in the 1979 All-Star Game after being named as a reserve

If Houston and Montreal stay on top, it will be the first time the National League play-offs take place entirely outside the United States.

> —HANK GREENWALD, sportscaster, on the 1979 pennant race

I had my bad days on the field, but I didn't take them home with me. I left them in a bar along the way.

> —BOB LEMON, reminiscing about his playing days

The Lord is all the glory. How else can you explain a mediocre shortstop playing in the World Series?

> —TIM FOLI, Pirates shortstop, celebrating their 1979 World Championship

Billy Martin and George Steinbrenner struck a temporary truce during their well-publicized 1978 squabbles. "The way our country's going," said Billy Martin, "maybe we'd be better off with me and George running it. I'd handle Russia and he'd handle China."

After all, I don't think God really cares about baseball. He's got more important things on his mind.

—DAN QUISENBERRY, relief pitcher

THE BRONX CIRCUS

When I was a little boy, I wanted to be a baseball player and join the circus. With the Yankees I've accomplished both.

—GRAIG NETTLES

Some people say you have to be crazy to be a reliever. Well, I don't know. I was crazy before I became one.

—SPARKY LYLE

Why pitch nine innings when you can get just as famous pitching two?

—SPARKY LYLE

If the Yankees want somebody to play third base, they've got me. If they want someone to attend banquets, they can get George Jessel.

—GRAIG NETTLES, after being fined for missing a boosters luncheon

It's become a contest. You gotta drink just to stay around here.

　　　　　　　—SPARKY LYLE

The sun don't shine on the same dog's ass all the time.

　　　　　　　—CATFISH HUNTER, after being defeated in a
　　　　　　　1977 World Series game

What every fan thinks is thrilling about the game, Thurman was part of, some way—a ninth inning hit to win the ball game, a slide in to home to beat somebody up. Knock them over, knock the ball loose, block the plate, throw somebody out! Thurman was always in the middle of it.

　　　　　　　—RICK DEMPSEY, recalling Thurman Munson

This is the thing the Yankees needed to make a dynasty.

　　　　　　　—RICH GOSSAGE, on his signing with New
　　　　　　　York

He went from Cy Young to sayonara in a year.

　　　　　　　—GRAIG NETTLES, on Sparky Lyle, after the
　　　　　　　award-winning reliever was traded to Texas
　　　　　　　following the 1978 season

I didn't come to New York to be a star. I brought my star with me.

　　　　　　　—REGGIE JACKSON

This team, it all flows from me. I've got to keep it all going. I'm the straw that stirs the drink. It all comes back to me. Maybe I should say me and Munson. But really he doesn't enter into it.

　　　　　　　—REGGIE JACKSON

Reggie Jackson's friends are those who tell him how good he is.

　　　　　　　—THURMAN MUNSON

He doesn't want to be recognized, he wants to be idolized.

　　　　　　　—SPARKY LYLE, on Reggie Jackson

Love me or hate me, you can't ignore me.

　　　　　　　—REGGIE JACKSON

I'm a one-year manager only if the front office interferes with my running the club. If it leaves me alone, I'm a twenty-year manager.

—BILLY MARTIN

Steinbrenner has one of the most expensive toys in the world and what he does is manipulate people. . . . Steinbrenner won't let anybody relax. It's what I call his corporate mentality. He throws a fear into everybody. . . . He makes the players fear for their jobs. That's his theory and it works.

—TONY KUBEK

There are two things George Steinbrenner doesn't know about: baseball and weight control.

—GRAIG NETTLES

George is a spoiled brat. If he doesn't like me as a cleanup hitter, let him go and buy a replacement.

—REGGIE JACKSON

It's a good thing Babe Ruth still isn't here. If he was, George would have him bat seventh and say he's overweight.

—GRAIG NETTLES

If Steinbrenner says, "Jump in a lake," he thinks you're supposed to do it.

—CATFISH HUNTER

They say I'm tough to work for. Well, I am, but I'm not trying to win any popularity contest. I know only one way, and that is to work my butt off and demand everybody else do the same.

—GEORGE STEINBRENNER

1. THE BOSS IS ALWAYS RIGHT.
2. IF THE BOSS IS WRONG, SEE NO. 1.

> —Sign hung in Billy Martin's office when he managed the Yankees

The rules are made by me, but I don't have to follow them.

—BILLY MARTIN

If Martin wins, he can take the credit, but if he loses, he'll have to take the blame.

　　　　　　　—GEORGE STEINBRENNER

George understands me. He's a businessman. Billy doesn't understand that. He's only a baseball manager.

　　　　　　　—REGGIE JACKSON

The two of them deserve each other. One's a born liar, the other's convicted.

　　　　　　　—BILLY MARTIN, on Reggie Jackson and George Steinbrenner

10

BIG BATS, BIG BUCKS, BIG MOUTHS:
The Game Today

○ THESE DAYS, so much of the action seems to take place off the field. Players want freedom. Owners demand compensation. Players want millions. Owners think salaries are too high. Attorneys, advisors, agents and negotiators are called in. Owners say they're losing money. Players want to see the books. Players call for a strike. Owners stand firm. Meanwhile, as usual, fans get the shaft. At the risk of appearing uncivil, one response to these enormously complex issues comes to mind: "Aw, shut up and play ball!"

REGGIE! REGGIE! REGGIE!

I don't want to be a hero. I don't want to be a star. It just works out that way.

—REGGIE JACKSON

Anything that has to do with Reggie Jackson becomes a big thing.

—REGGIE JACKSON

Reggie hits the second of three home runs to lead the Yankees over the Dodgers in the final game of the 1977 World Series. The next day Bill Lee was asked to assess the impact of Jackson's epic performance. "I think there are going to be a lot of Reggies born in this town," he said.

I represent both the underdog and the overdog in this society. It's not really an athlete's story. It is a human story.

—REGGIE JACKSON

Reggie's a really good guy, down deep he is. . . . He'd give you the shirt off his back. Of course, he'd call a press conference to announce it.

—CATFISH HUNTER, teammate at both Oakland and New York

There's Reggie Jackson lovers and Reggie Jackson haters. I don't think he cares which way they go as long as they shout, "Reggie!"

—BILLY HUNTER

I don't want to be liked, I just want to be respected.

—REGGIE JACKSON

I love competition. It motivates me, stimulates me, excites me. It is almost sexual. I just love to hit that baseball in a big game.

—REGGIE JACKSON

Late in a close big game—and with the deep, baying cries from the stands rolling across the field: "Reg-gie! Reg-gie! Reg-gie!"—he strides to the plate and taps it with his bat and settles his batting helmet and gets his feet right and turns his glittery regard toward the pitcher, and we suddenly know that it is a different hitter we are watching now, and a different man. Get ready, everybody—it's show time.

—ROGER ANGELL

The only reason I don't like playing in the World Series is I can't watch myself play.

—REGGIE JACKSON

The advantage of playing in New York is in getting to watch Reggie Jackson play every day. And the disadvantage is in getting to watch Reggie Jackson play every day.

—GRAIG NETTLES

I was in a position where, if I failed, the fans and the press would have buried me. They getcha, boy. They don't let you escape with minor scratches and bruises. They put scars on you here. Come to the Big Apple and have a bite. I had to either learn to digest, or choke.

—REGGIE JACKSON

The circus is back in town.

—RICK CERONE, welcoming Jackson to the
Yankees' training camp

136

When everything is in place, in the proper sequence, he's awesome. In a season of four hundred and fifty at bats, maybe twelve hundred swings, you can only count on maybe twenty perfect swings a year. When he does it, I get goose pimples.

> —CHARLEY LAU, Yankee batting coach, on watching Jackson hit

Babe Ruth was great. I was only lucky.

> —REGGIE JACKSON

Taters, that's where the money is.

> —REGGIE JACKSON

Reggie Jackson hit one off me that's still burrowing its way to Los Angeles.

> —DAN QUISENBERRY

There is nobody who can put meat in the seats the way I can.

> —REGGIE JACKSON

Nothing can happen to me because I can hit the ball over the wall. When I can't hit the ball over the wall, they'll get me too. George will get me someday.

> —REGGIE JACKSON

THE FAST PHILLIES

If the Food and Drug Administration ever walked into the Phils' clubhouse, they'd close down baseball.

> —TUG MCGRAW

Tug McGraw has got about forty-eight cards in his deck.

> —TOM SEAVER

Sometimes I hit him like I used to hit Sandy Koufax, and that's like drinking coffee with a fork.

> —WILLIE STARGELL, on facing Steve Carlton

When you call a pitcher "Lefty" and everybody in both leagues knows who you mean, he must be pretty good.

> —CLINT HURDLE

Steve Carlton won twenty-four games in 1980 to lead the Phillies to their first pennant in thirty years. Asked what the Royals planned to do against Carlton in the Series, Frank White, their second baseman, said, "We'll have to lay off the low slider, hit the fastball, and hope he gets up on the wrong side of the bed."

I think Lefty could win twenty games pitching to a backstop.
—TIM MCCARVER

With the money I'm making, I should be playing two positions.
—PETE ROSE

Pete doesn't count his money anymore. He weighs it.
—STAN MUSIAL

Pete Rose has a twelve-year-old heart inside a thirty-eight-year-old body.
—TUG MCGRAW

I always say, the only time you gotta worry about getting booed is when you're wearing a white uniform. And I've never been booed wearing a white uniform.
—PETE ROSE

I'd walk through hell in a gasoline suit to keep playing baseball.
—PETE ROSE

When I was a kid, I always tried to crush the ball. I guess I'm still trying.

—MIKE SCHMIDT

Mike wants to hit it all the way out of the stadium, not just three hundred and thirty feet over the outfield fence. With his swing, he can hit twenty accidentally.

—LARRY BOWA, Phils shortstop

They'd always said I thought too much. But what people don't realize is that the game of baseball can just reach out, grab you and humble you. A hundred years ago someone . . . put the pitcher's rubber sixty feet six inches from home plate. Six inches closer and the curve ball doesn't have enough time to break; six inches farther back and it breaks too soon. Now you're going to tell me that this game doesn't deserve a great deal of thought?

—MIKE SCHMIDT

The earth is two-thirds covered by water, and the other one-third is covered by Garry Maddox.

—RALPH KINER

He's turned his life around. He used to be depressed and miserable. Now he's miserable and depressed.

—HARRY KALAS, sportscaster, on center fielder Garry Maddox

If there's something you want to do, I mean really bad, you can do it if you sacrifice. I may be kicked in the face, but I'll be damned if I'm going to quit.

—LARRY BOWA

This is the end of an incredible journey. I get the feeling that W. C. Fields is out of his grave tonight celebrating with us. I gotta believe that even old Ben Franklin is turning over in his grave.

—TUG McGRAW, celebrating the Phils' 1980 World Championship

New York can take this World Championship and stick it!

—TUG McGRAW

BALL PARK CHATTER

All winter long, I can't wait for baseball. It gets you back to doing the stuff you love and makes you wish the youthfulness of life could stay with you forever.

—TOMMY JOHN

In the competition for the spring training optimism award, all twenty-six teams are tied for first.

—SCOTT OSTLER, sportswriter

George Brett. "The small boy does not know that the best third baseman in baseball is human. . . . All the small boy knows is that the third baseman is his hero, and a hero always does the right thing" —Robert W. Creamer.

I've never been wrong yet. They just didn't execute what I wanted them to do.

> —CHUCK TANNER, Pirates manager

I found a delivery in my flaw.

> —DAN QUISENBERRY, on why he was having
> pitching problems

I don't see how anyone can criticize a player of my ability and attitude.

> —AL OLIVER

There are two theories on hitting the knuckleball. Unfortunately, neither of them works.

> —CHARLEY LAU

Players like rules. If they didn't have any rules, they wouldn't have anything to break.

> —LEE WALLS, A's coach

Between owners and players, a manager today has become a wishbone.

> —JOHN CURTIS, pitcher

I think they recycle more managers than cans.

> —BILLY NORTH

I think Ray Kroc told 'em to give the job to Gary Coleman and they misunderstood him.

> —JERRY COLEMAN, on how he became the
> Padres' manager in 1980. He lasted one season
> on the job, then returned to the announcing
> booth.

Me and my owners think exactly alike. Whatever they're thinking, that's what I'm thinking.

> —JIM FREGOSI. On one matter, however,
> Fregosi and his owners weren't in accord; he
> was fired as Angels manager at the start of the
> '81 season.

The worst thing about managing is the day you realize you want to win more than the players do.

—GENE MAUCH

The difference between Earl Weaver and Gene Mauch is that Weaver believes in platooning as a strategy and Mauch believes in platooning as a religion.

—Anonymous

Some guys throw to spots, some to zones. Renie throws to continents.

—DAN QUISENBERRY, on reliever Renie Martin

I remember one pitcher, a blond left-hander. Thought he belonged in Hollywood. He didn't report for practice one day, and I asked him what's the problem. The guy said he had to finish the scenario he was writing.

—BURT SHOTTON, recalling his days as manager of the hapless 1930 Phillies

When we played, World Series checks meant something. Now all they do is screw up your taxes.

—DON DRYSDALE

You know, just because I'm making a new salary, am I supposed to play better?

—DAVE WINFIELD

Dave [Kingman] has the personality of a tree trunk. He's not a bad guy, but if you try to talk to him, about all he does is grunt.

—JOHN STEARNS, teammate of Kingman's on the Mets

Kingman's home address is Disabled List, U.S.A.

—DICK YOUNG

The best thing the press can do for me is give me peace and quiet.

—DAVE KINGMAN

Mike Ivie is a forty million dollar airport with a thirty dollar control tower.

—RICK MONDAY

142

The Angels' Rod Carew, says Alan Bannister, is "the only guy I know who can go four for three."

Claudell Washington plays the outfield like he's trying to catch grenades.

      —REGGIE JACKSON

I don't want to be a star. Stars get blamed too much.

      —ENOS CABELL

INTERVIEWER: *Now that you're thirty-five, and in the twilight of your career, how much longer do you hope to play for the Giants?*
MIKE SADEK: *As long as I can be of value to them . . . and three years more.*

It's a mere moment in a man's life between an All-Star Game and an old-timer's game.

      —VIN SCULLY, sportscaster

What's one home run? If you hit one, they are just going to want you to hit two.

      —MICK KELLEHER, infielder, who has never hit a major league home run

Baseball regards umpires as a necessary evil. If they could play games without umpires, I'm sure the majority would vote to do so.

> —HARRY WENDELSTEDT, umpire

One day we woke up and the Wicked Witch of the North was dead and we were all the children of Oz.

> —MATT KEOUGH, Oakland pitcher, on the sale of the A's by Charlie Finley to new owners

He is the guts of the Angels, our triple threat. He can hit, run and lob.

> —MERV RETTENMUND, Angels coach, on sore-armed outfielder Don Baylor

Watching Fernando Valenzuela force himself into a Dodger uniform is like seeing Kate Smith struggling to fit into a pair of Brooke Shields' designer jeans.

> —H. G. REZA (Early in the 1981 season the Mexican-born left-hander was asked if he thought he had a chance for the Cy Young award. "What's that?" asked Fernando.)

Jerry Reuss pitched the majors' only no-hitter in 1980. After the game Dodger manager Tom Lasorda, a former pitcher himself, said, "It couldn't have happened to a nicer guy. Well, yes it could. I could have pitched it."

It is good for the Dodgers. It is good for baseball. It is good for Mexico. It is good for our relations with Mexico. And it is very good for Tommy Lasorda.

> —TOMMY LASORDA, on what Fernando
> Valenzuela means to him

Tradition in St. Louis is Stan Musial coming into the clubhouse and making the rounds. Tradition in San Diego is Nate Colbert coming into the clubhouse and trying to sell a used car.

> —BOB SHIRLEY, former Padres pitcher traded
> to the Cards in 1980

We have a good bench. The trouble is, the bench is on the field.

> —Cubs player, assessing his team before the
> season

The Cubs are like what they used to say about Austria: serious, but not hopeless.

> —BRUCE MORTON. Another joke about the
> Cubbies involves a radio announcer, who
> makes an emergency plea over the air: "Will
> the lady who lost her nine children at Wrigley
> Field please pick them up immediately? They
> are beating the Cubs ten to nothing in the
> seventh."

The Cubs are into their thirty-sixth rebuilding year.

> —JOE GODDARD, sportswriter (1981)

I believe in the Rip Van Winkle theory—that a man from 1910 must be able to wake up after being asleep for seventy years, walk into a ball park, and understand baseball perfectly.

> —BOWIE KUHN

If I hear Bowie Kuhn say just once more he's doing something for the betterment of baseball, I'm going to throw up.

> —SPARKY ANDERSON

Bowie is the best commissioner in baseball today.

> —JIM BOUTON

The fans come to see me strike out, hit a home run or run into a fence. I try to accommodate them at least one way every game.

—GORMAN THOMAS, Brewers outfielder

The nice thing about César Cedeño is that he can play all three outfield positions—at the same time.

—GENE MAUCH

I'm basically a normal pitcher if there's no pressure. But with the game on the line, I go crazy. . . . My whole personality changes.

—RICH GOSSAGE, Yankee reliever

Look at Gossage. He's six feet four and most of it is fat. He pitches maybe an inning a week. And for that, they pay him a million dollars a year. And you know what? He's worth it.

—RUDY MAY. Asked to compare himself with Gossage, Dan Quisenberry said, "I don't like being compared to a guy who throws harder than God."

He has me O and two before I ever get in the box.

—JERRY REMY, infielder, on what it's like to face Jim Palmer

It takes him an hour and a half to watch "60 Minutes."

—DONALD DAVIDSON, on the easygoing style of pitcher Joe Niekro

Being traded is like celebrating your hundredth birthday. It might not be the happiest occasion in the world, but consider the alternatives.

—JOE GARAGIOLA

When they operated on my arm, I asked them to put in a Koufax fastball. They did. But it was a Mrs. Koufax fastball.

—TOMMY JOHN

Every team needs a foundation, and I'm it. Just look at me. They ought to pay me just to walk around here.

—DAVE PARKER, Pirates slugger

Willie Wilson came up to bat 705 times in 1980, rapped 230 hits and stole 79 bases. Gene Mauch said he is "the most disruptive productive concentration-breaker in baseball."

My approach is: see something I like and attack it.

—DAVE PARKER

REPORTER *(after an impressive win by Jim Kaat):* You really fooled them with your change-up.

JIM KAAT: *That wasn't my change-up. That was my fastball.*

I sincerely think that I was born to be a Dodger.

—STEVE GARVEY

God has laid out the game plan. I walk around as if a little boy or a little girl was following me and I don't do anything physically or mentally to take away from the ideal they might have for Steve Garvey.

—STEVE GARVEY

Steve Garvey can't help it if he's perfect.

—Inscription on fan's T-shirt

I believe there are certain things that cannot be bought: loyalty, friendship, health, love and an American League pennant.

> —EDWARD BENNETT WILLIAMS, chairman of
> the board of the Baltimore Orioles, on why his
> team doesn't get involved in free agent bidding

There's no pressure playing ball. This is lots of fun. Pressure is when you have to go to the unemployment office to pick up a check to support four people.

> —GEORGE BRETT

George Brett could get good wood on an aspirin.

> —JIM FREY

If God had him no balls and two strikes, he'd still get a hit.

> —STEVE PALERMO, umpire, on George Brett

He hits better than any white man I've ever seen. As a matter of fact, Brett hits so good he hits like a black man.

> —AL OLIVER

All my problems are behind me.

> —GEORGE BRETT, discussing the fabled case of
> hemorrhoids that temporarily forced him out
> of the 1980 Series

Oscar Gamble is so old that when he broke into the major leagues he was a Negro.

> —STAN WILLIAMS

I flush the john between innings to keep my wrists strong.

> —JOHN LOWENSTEIN, designated hitter, on how
> he keeps ready while on the bench

Bill Buckner had a nineteen-game hitting streak going [in 1980] and always wore the same underwear. Of course, he didn't have any friends.

> —LENNY RANDLE, a teammate of Buckner's
> that year on the Cubs

I've been roasted so much this winter I feel like a chicken.

> —PETE ROSE, after an off-season on the
> banquet circuit

Jim Rice is tagged out by the Brewers' Ray Fosse in a close play at the plate. "It may be that baseball is, under close analysis, pointless. What seems apparent to me is that close analysis is pointless. The game is there. It is the best game there is. That's all I need to know"—Art Hill.

Chuck Tanner used to have a bedcheck just for me every night. No problem. My bed was always there.

> —JIM ROOKER, reminiscing on his late-night rambling when he pitched for the Pirates

If the human body recognized agony and frustration, people would never run marathons, have babies or play baseball.

> —CARLTON FISK

THREE MANAGERS:
LASORDA, MARTIN, WEAVER

Bad ballplayers make good managers.

—EARL WEAVER

Relief pitchers today are asked to make more appearances than ever before. But so what? If one burns his arm out, you buy another one.

—EARL WEAVER

I believe if God had ever managed, He would have been very aggressive, the way I manage.

—BILLY MARTIN

Never take shit from nobody.

—JENNY DOWNEY, Billy Martin's mother

You wouldn't hold up Billy Martin to your sons as an example of what kind of person you'd want them to be, except as an example of how to win.

—Anonymous sportswriter

There's no excuse for happy losers.

—BILLY MARTIN

Cut me and I'll bleed Dodger blue.

—TOM LASORDA

When I die I want my tombstone to say, "Dodger Stadium was his address, but every ball park was his home."

—TOM LASORDA

TOM LASORDA (during a 1968 press conference): *I want to continue working for the Dodgers even when I'm dead and gone.*
WALTER O'MALLEY: *And just how do you plan to do that?*
TOM LASORDA: *Just put the Dodgers' schedule on [my tombstone] every year. When people are visiting their loved ones at the cemetery, they can come by my grave and see if the Dodgers are at home or away.*

I was leery of Tommy at first. I believe in God, not the Big Dodger in the Sky.

—DON SUTTON

Managing is like holding a dove in your hand. Squeeze too hard and you kill it; not hard enough and it flies away.

—TOM LASORDA

Out of twenty-five guys there should be fifteen who would run through a wall for you, two or three who don't like you at all, five who are indifferent and maybe three undecided. My job is to keep the last two groups from going the wrong way.

—BILLY MARTIN, expressing ideas very similar to those of his mentor, Casey Stengel

INTERVIEWER: *What's the secret to managing?*
EARL WEAVER: *Get the guy up there you want.*

All it is, I work the three-to-eleven shift.

—EARL WEAVER

When I get through managing, I'm going to open up a kindergarten.

—BILLY MARTIN

Billy Martin is the first manager I ever had who didn't need my help.

—CHARLIE O. FINLEY

Billy likes the odds. People think he can't do something and he proves he can.

—CLETE BOYER

Billy Martin. "His intensity is unique. Under the cap, his face is pale and tight, and he looks almost ill with concentration and hostility. . . . It is the face of a man in a street fight, a man up an alley when the knives have just come out. It is win or die"—Roger Angell.

When you're a professional, you come back, no matter what happened the day before.

—BILLY MARTIN

PAT KELLY: *When was the last time you read the Bible, Earl?*
EARL WEAVER: *After my father's funeral.*
PAT KELLY: *And when was the last time you were on your knees?*
EARL WEAVER: *The last time I sent you up to pinch-hit.*

Kell told me one time after he hit a home run that the Lord was looking out for him. I said, yeah, and what about that poor sonuvabitch on the mound who threw you the high slider? We better not be counting on God. I ain't got no stats on God.

—EARL WEAVER

PAT KELLY: *You've got to walk with the Lord, Skip.*
EARL WEAVER: *Kell, I'd rather you walk with the bases loaded.*

When you say you're a Padre, people ask when did you become a parent. When you say you're a Cardinal, they tell you to work hard because the next step is Pope. But when you say you're a Dodger, everybody knows you're in the major leagues.

—TOM LASORDA

You could plant two thousand rows of corn with the fertilizer Lasorda spreads around.

—JOE GARAGIOLA

Every year Tommy offers fifty thousand dollars to the family of the Unknown Soldier.

—DON SUTTON

When Billy Martin reaches for a bar tab, his arm shrinks six inches.

—TOM LASORDA

I discovered one thing, finally, about Billy. His job is not to like me; his job is to do anything he can to get me to win baseball games.

—MIKE NORRIS

152

"I read every newspaper I can get my hands on from front to back," says Tommy Lasorda. "And in the business I'm in, that includes the classifieds for unemployment."

You can't sit on a lead and run a few plays into the line and just kill the clock. You've got to throw the ball over the goddamn plate and give the other man his chance. That's why baseball is the greatest game of them all.

—EARL WEAVER

BASEBALL STRIKES OUT

As far as we're concerned, this baseball season [1981] is a wipeout. What began as one of the most glittering seasons in years has been tarnished beyond repair by the players' strike. . . . Baseball will be a long time recovering from this self-inflicted wound.

—The Sporting News

Major league baseball will not be able to look itself in the mirror or take pride in what it has performed for the public. . . . In 1981 the game merely hurled itself on its sword.

—BILL CONLIN, sportswriter

The strike is going to hurt the game. Many people will find other things to do, and once they get away, they may not come back.

—DWIGHT EVANS, Red Sox outfielder

Earl Weaver makes a point with ump Bill Haller.
"The Umpire has the awesome power
To send a grown man to the shower,
Yet cannot, in the aftermath,
Coerce his kids to take a bath."
—Bob McKenty

I don't question their [the players'] right to have a union, but I'm constitutionally opposed to strikes against the government and strikes against baseball. This strike is against the American people, and they're not entitled to do that.

—ALBERT "HAPPY" CHANDLER, former
commissioner of baseball

Just when my Chicago Cubs win three straight, this baseball strike has to start. . . . I am sore enough to say, why not tell the players to get back on the field, or we'll hire replacements?

—NICK THIMMESCH, columnist

I think the fans are important, but they're no different than any other consumers inconvenienced by a strike. If the sanitation workers strike, consumers are inconvenienced and annoyed, but that doesn't give the fans the right to say the players may not protect themselves.

—MARVIN MILLER

It's absurd for pundits . . . to say that this owner or that owner should sit down with the players and settle this thing. Owners have individual selfish interest. Each owner, given the chance, would be inclined to do what is best for him; not for the common good, not for the game, certainly not for the fan.

—DICK YOUNG

The basic issue of the strike is how the owners and players will divide the pie that the fans make possible.

—NOEL FALES, fan

The national pastime has caught the national disease—the irresponsible, exploitative and plain dumb abuse of delicate institutions.

—GEORGE F. WILL, columnist

We've got a commissioner who doesn't represent both sides. He doesn't even know who's playing the game. I've been introduced to him eight or nine times over the years and every time he says, "Nice to meet you."

—BUDDY BELL, Rangers third baseman

The strike would never have happened if Judge Landis or Bowie Kuhn were alive today.

—RED SMITH

It's like when your mother tells you to do something and you don't want to do it. Then she tells you, "There are a lot of things in life you don't want to do, but you have to do them." That's the way I feel about the strike.

—DON COOPER, pitcher

I kinda look at the strike as a long rainout.

—JIM PALMER

Everyone is losing in this strike, whether it's the fans, the players, the owners and even the nation as a whole. When you get right down to it, the really sad thing is that no one is winning.

—KEN GRIFFEY, outfielder

I don't care who wins the strike and I don't care what the issues are. I see the strike mostly as a fight between two groups of rich men on the country club veranda, greed trying to throw a hammerlock on more greed. . . . I don't care who wins the fight because the fight is a colossal bore. I just want baseball.

—LEIGH MONTVILLE, sportswriter

11
BASEBALL'S GREATEST FLAKES

O JIMMY PIERSALL hits a home run and runs the bases backwards. While talking to a reporter, Babe Herman casually pulls a lit cigar from his pocket and starts smoking it. After his wife returns from seeing *Doctor Zhivago*, Yogi Berra asks her, "What, are you sick again?" Gee Walker is picked off second base and explains to his manager, "I was tapping my foot and they caught me between taps." Why are there so many screwballs in baseball? Peter Gent has an explanation: "It's all that organ music."

The way to catch a knuckleball is to wait until the ball stops rolling and then pick it up.

—BOB UECKER, former catcher

REPORTER: *How did you like school when you were growing up, Yogi?*
YOGI BERRA: *Closed.*

Kids should practice autographing baseballs. This is a skill that's often overlooked in Little League.

—TUG MCGRAW

157

Dan Bankhead, spring training, 1951. "Baseball is a circus, and as is the case in many a circus, the clowns and the sideshows are frequently more interesting than the big stuff in the main tent"
—W. O. McGeehan.

Tonight we're honoring one of the all-time greats in baseball, Stan Musial. He's immoral.

> —JOHNNY LOGAN, former shortstop turned sportscaster, speaking at an awards banquet

REPORTER: *How do you like playing in Montreal, Bill?*
BILL LEE: *Once I get past customs, everything's fine.*

A flake is a natural thing from the clouds.

> —GEORGE THEODORE

When Neil Armstrong first set foot on the moon, he and all the space scientists were puzzled by an unidentifiable white object. I knew immediately what it was. That was a home run ball hit off me in 1937 by Jimmie Foxx.

> —LEFTY GOMEZ

Baseball is a fun game. It beats working for a living.

> —PHIL LINZ, former Yankees shortstop

LEFTY GOMEZ: *What's your cap size, Yogi?*
YOGI BERRA: *How do I know? I'm not in shape yet.*

DOOR-TO-DOOR SALESMAN: *Babe, how would you like to buy a set of encyclopedias for your home? They'll help your kids with their education.*

BABE HERMAN: *Nothing doing. My kids can walk to school like I did.*

There are three things the average man thinks he can do better than anybody else: Build a fire, run a hotel and manage a baseball team.

—ROCKY BRIDGES, minor league manager

Rocky Bridges chews tobacco because the chewing gum industry wants no part of him.

—DON RICKLES

I will perish this forever.

—JOHNNY LOGAN, accepting an award

KEN BOSWELL: *I'm in a rut. I can't break myself of this habit. I keep swinging up at the ball.*

YOGI BERRA: *Well, swing down.*

Some guys have grace under pressure, some have dignity, but Tug McGraw has flake under pressure.

—VIN SCULLY

REPORTER: *What are you going to do with your World Series share, Tug?*

TUG MCGRAW: *Ninety percent of it I'll spend on whiskey, women and other good times. The other 10 percent I'll probably waste.*

Happiness is a first-class pad, good wheels, an understanding manager, and a little action.

—BO BELINSKY

I don't know why, but I can run faster in tight pants.

—PHIL LINZ

I've got a new invention. It's a revolving bowl for tired goldfish.

—LEFTY GOMEZ

159

*When cerebral processes enter into sports, you start screwing up.
It's like the Constitution, which says separate church and state.
You have to separate mind and body.*

—BILL LEE

When you start thinkin' is when you get your ass beat.

—SPARKY LYLE

*I think a lot of relief pitchers develop a crazy facade. . . . Of
course, maybe it's only the crazies that want to be relief pitchers.*

—SKIP LOCKWOOD, relief pitcher

REPORTER: *What do you plan to do after the Series is over, Dan?*
DAN QUISENBERRY: *I'm looking forward to putting on my
glasses with the fake nose so I can walk around and be a normal
person.*

Ninety percent of this game is half mental.

—JIM WOHLFORD, utilityman

*You've got to be very careful if you don't know where you are
going, because you might not get there.*

—YOGI BERRA

Bill Lee, aka The
Spaceman, was asked
why left-handers were
always considered
flakes. He said,
"Well, what do you
expect from a
northpaw world?"

TOM SEAVER: *Hey, Yogi, what time is it?*
YOGI BERRA: *You mean now?*

I just found out what's driving me crazy—it's baseball.
                              —RON TAYLOR, one-time Mets pitcher

REPORTER: *That was a close play at second base. Why didn't you slide?*
FRENCHY BORDAGARAY: *Because I didn't want to break the cigars in my pocket.*

There is one word in America that says it all, and that one word is "You never know."
                              —JOAQUÍN ANDUJAR, Dominican-born pitcher

I think Little League is wonderful. It keeps the kids out of the house.

                              —YOGI BERRA

I was only in the majors two months before I got a raise. The minimum went up.
                              —BOB UECKER

Anybody with ability can play in the big leagues. But to be able to trick people year in and year out the way I did, I think that was a much greater feat.
                              —BOB UECKER

They shouldn't throw at me. I'm the father of five or six kids.
                              —TITO FUENTES, after being brushed back by a
                              pitch

LEFTY GOMEZ: *I talked to the ball lots of times during my career.*
REPORTER: *What did you say to it?*
LEFTY GOMEZ: *Go foul, go foul.*

In baseball, you're supposed to sit on your ass, spit tobacco and nod at stupid things.
                              —BILL LEE

Play me or keep me.
                              —PHIL LINZ

161

I remember one time I'm batting against the Dodgers in Milwaukee. They lead, two to one, it's the bottom of the ninth, bases loaded for us, two out and the pitcher has a full count on me. I look over to the Dodger dugout, and they're all in street clothes.

—BOB UECKER

I don't need an agent. Why should I give somebody ten percent when I do all the work?

—MARK FIDRYCH

A nickel ain't worth a dime anymore.

—YOGI BERRA

You have two hemispheres in your brain—a left and a right side. The left side controls the right side of your body and the right controls the left half. It's a fact. Therefore, left-handers are the only people in their right minds.

—BILL LEE

How can I intimidate batters if I look like a goddamn golf pro?

—AL "THE MAD HUNGARIAN" HRABOSKY, on being asked to shave his facial hair

You can't get rich sitting on the bench—but I'm giving it a try.

—PHIL LINZ

TRAFFIC COP (pulling Phil Linz over for a violation): *Your driver's license says you wear glasses. Why aren't you wearing them?*
PHIL LINZ: *I got contacts.*
TRAFFIC COP: *I don't care who you know, you still have to wear glasses when you drive.*

We're all sad to see Glenn Beckert leave. Before he goes, though, I hope he stops by so we can kiss him good-bye. He's that kind of guy.

—JERRY COLEMAN, broadcaster

We've got an absolutely perfect day here at Desert Sun Stadium, and we're told it's going to be even more perfect tomorrow.

—JERRY COLEMAN

Tigers pitcher Mark Fidrych once returned a ball to an ump after he'd given up a hit with it. His reason: "Well, that ball had a hit in it, so I wanted it to get back in the ball bag and goof around with the other balls there. Maybe it'll learn some sense and come out a pop-up next time."

There's someone warming up in the bull pen, but he's obscured by his number.

    —JERRY COLEMAN

With one out here in the first, Dave Roberts looks a lot better than the last time he pitched against the Padres.

    —JERRY COLEMAN

I played for Washington five different times. That beat Franklin Delano Roosevelt's record. He was only elected four times.

    —BOBO NEWSOM

BLUE JAY PLAYER: *Hey, Jackie, did you know that John Kenneth Galbraith is on the same flight we are?*

JACKIE MOORE: *Oh yeah, I remember him. Short guy, mustache, played third base for Pittsburgh.*

Mike Anderson's limitations are limitless.

    —DANNY OZARK, former Phillies manager, on one of his outfielders

Natural grass is a wonderful thing for little bugs and sinkerball pitchers.

    —DAN QUISENBERRY

Marvelous Marv Throneberry, calamity-prone first baseman, was called out on a triple for failing to touch first base. "How could he be expected to remember where the bases were?" said Jack Lang. "He gets on so infrequently."

INTERVIEWER: *I understand you had an audience with the Pope.*
YOGI BERRA: *No, but I saw him.*
INTERVIEWER: *Did you get to talk to him?*
YOGI BERRA: *I sure did. We had a nice little chat.*
INTERVIEWER: *What did he say?*
YOGI BERRA: *Ya know, he must read the papers a lot, because he said, "Hello, Yogi."*
INTERVIEWER: *And what did you say?*
YOGI BERRA: *I said, "Hello, Pope."*

"I don't like to make a big deal about my job," says reliever Dan Quisenberry. "I'm just a garbage man. I come into a game and clean up other people's mess."

Yogi Berra, wonderful Yogi, was once introduced to writer Ernest Hemingway. Said Yogi, rising to shake Hemingway's hand, "Yeah, what paper you write for, Ernie?"

If the people don't want to come out to the park, nobody's going to stop 'em.

> —YOGI BERRA, on declining attendance at a major league ball park

REPORTER: *Were you apprehensive in the twelfth inning?*
YOGI BERRA: *No, but I was scared.*

I'm a lucky guy, and I'm happy to be with the Yankees. And I want to thank everyone for making this night necessary.

> —YOGI BERRA, at a dinner in his honor

How can a guy think and hit at the same time?

> —YOGI BERRA

They say he's funny. Well, he has a lovely wife and family, a beautiful home, money in the bank, and he plays golf with millionaires. What's funny about that?

> —CASEY STENGEL, on Yogi Berra

12
BASEBALL IS EVERY-BODY'S BUSINESS
(or at least it ought to be)

O YOU KNOW who's to blame for the ongoing baseball strife, of course. Not Curt Flood, not the owners, not Bowie Kuhn, not the Messersmith decision, not lawyers, not agents, not Marvin Miller, not arbitration, not George Steinbrenner, not compensation or the lack of it, not Rennie Stennett (or Claudell Washington or any of the other nouveau riche), not the courts, not any of that. No, the real culprit here is Al Reach who, in 1864, became the first person to openly accept money for playing ball. He's the guy who got us into this mess!

Baseball is too much of a sport to be called a business, and too much of a business to be called a sport.
                                                                —PHILIP WRIGLEY

Is baseball a business? If it isn't, General Motors is a sport.

—JIM MURRAY

Baseball is show business. How do you think we average thirty-two thousand a game here? We've got stars, that's how.

—GEORGE STEINBRENNER

Money chasing is the great American game. Professional baseball is based on money chasing.

—JOHN B. SHERIDAN (1922)

The fact that the [owners] produce baseball games as a source of profit, large or small, cannot change the character of the games. They are still sport, not trade.

—District of Columbia Court of Appeal (1921)

It's a business. If I could make more money down in the zinc mines, I'd be mining zinc.

—ROGER MARIS

That we receive larger salaries and that our hours of work are shorter leaves us none the less workingmen. We are hired men, skilled in a particular employment, who work not only for the profit, but for the amusement of our employers.

—JOHN MONTGOMERY WARD, Hall-of-Fame
pitcher and shortstop (1887)

Athletes are pieces of meat. No matter who you are, the second your ability to produce is not up to what they expect it to be, you're disposable.

—DAVE KINGMAN

You measure the value of a ballplayer by how many fannies he puts in the seats.

—GEORGE STEINBRENNER

Being an owner is like being a giraffe. You're always sticking your neck out whether you want to or not.

—Anonymous owner

I can make more money out of one hamburger stand than I can out of baseball.

—RAY KROC, owner of the Padres and founder of the McDonald's empire

I'm going to write a book, How to Make a Small Fortune in Baseball. *First, you start with a large fortune. . . .*

—RULY CARPENTER, Phillies owner

This club is a lot of fun, like my wife, but there's no profit in either one.

—RAY KROC

The crack of the bat striking the ball in modern baseball is drowned out by the noises of the owners yelling about money.

—JIMMY CANNON

The last people who went broke in baseball were Roy and Earle Mack, Connie's sons. And I claim they did it on merit.

—RED SMITH

No business in the world has ever made more money with poorer management.

—BILL TERRY (1941)

Baseball has always chosen the longest way around and never been administered with real intelligence.

—PAUL GALLICO

Baseball must be a great game to survive the fools who run it.

—BILL TERRY

No court in the world can make a Gene Autry or a George Steinbrenner give a player three million dollars. The courts cocked the gun. It's the owners who pulled the trigger.

—RULY CARPENTER

When you come right down to it, the baseball owners are really little boys with big wallets.

—HAROLD PARROTT

In 1975 an arbitrator ruled that Andy Messersmith (above) and Dave McNally were no longer bound to their respective teams and could sell their talents to the highest bidder, thus ushering in the free agent era. "I am not an Abraham Lincoln signing the Emancipation Proclamation," said the arbitrator, Peter Seitz. "Involuntary servitude has nothing to do with this case. This decision does not destroy baseball."

If the owners didn't have it, they wouldn't be giving it, and if they want to give it, the players will take it.

—BILL CAMPBELL, pitcher

I didn't ask for the money, they offered it to me. No one was ever paid more than he was worth.

—WAYNE GARLAND, after signing with
Cleveland as a free agent in 1976

First the players wanted a hamburger and the owners gave them a hamburger. Then they wanted a filet mignon and they gave them a filet mignon. Then they wanted the whole damn cow, and now that they got the cow they want a pasture to put [it] in.

—RIP SEWELL

I used to be [among] the top five [salaried players]. Now I'm in the top forty. I feel like a record.

—JOHNNY BENCH

The handwriting is on the wall, but these athletes can't read.

—CHARLIE FINLEY

How can the manager exert discipline? What is he going to do to a guy with a million dollar contract, fine him?

—LEO DUROCHER

I'm the most loyal player money can buy.

—DON SUTTON

Players have lost all loyalty to a club, to their teammates and perhaps even to themselves.

—BUZZIE BAVASI, baseball executive

This loyalty stuff is a bunch of bull. Anybody should have a chance to make it while they can.

—WAYNE GARLAND

A man ought to get all he can earn. A man who knows he's making money for other people ought to get some of the profit he brings in. Don't make any difference if it's baseball or a bank or a vaudeville show.

—BABE RUTH

Champions cost money.

—CONNIE MACK. Mack broke up two championship teams, once in 1915 and again in 1923, because the salaries of his stars were too high.

It isn't the high price of stars that's expensive. It's the high price of mediocrity.

—BILL VEECK

We live by the Golden Rule. Those who have the gold make the rules.

—BUZZIE BAVASI

The owners are seeing what Hollywood saw a long time ago. Stars are worth a lot of money. They attract people. Hollywood paid these big salaries twenty years ago. Of course, Hollywood would pay the spear carriers scale. Baseball is paying the spear carriers as stars.

—REUVEN KATZ, players' agent

Bowie Kuhn, commissioner of baseball, citing skyrocketing players' salaries in the free agent era, said in 1981, "Barring the discovery of oil wells under second base, financial losses in the next five years will be nearly ten times greater than in the last five."

Isn't it amazing that we're worth so much on the trading block and worth so little when we talk salary with the general manager?

—JIM KERN, Rangers pitcher

Baseball as at present conducted is a gigantic monopoly, intolerant of opposition and run on a grab-all-there-is-in-sight policy that is alienating its friends and disgusting the very public that has so long and cheerfully given it . . . support.

—CAP ANSON, Hall-of-Fame infielder and one of the game's early stars (1900)

It is, in fact, quite possible for a big league club to go on forever without ever paying any income tax. . . . Look, we play "The Star Spangled Banner" before every game. You want us to pay income taxes, too?

—BILL VEECK

There was a time when the League stood for integrity and fair dealing; today it stands for dollars and cents. Once it looked to the elevation of the game and an honest exhibition of the sport. Today its eyes are upon the turnstile. Men have come into the business for no other motive than to exploit it for every dollar in sight.

—The Brotherhood Manifesto (1889). The Brotherhood of Ball Players was a group of big leaguers who, in protest over salaries and especially the reserve clause, formed their own league in 1890. The rebellion ended a year later when most of the players returned to the National League and the American Association.

Curt Flood, then a gifted center fielder for the Cardinals, objected to being traded to Philadelphia and filed a pioneering though ultimately unsuccessful lawsuit against baseball's reserve clause in early 1970. "I just decided that there comes a time in a man's life when he should have a say in where he goes to work," he said.

After twelve years of being in the major leagues, I do not feel I am a piece of property to be bought and sold irrespective of my wishes.

—CURT FLOOD (1969)

This year I was sold to Cleveland and told that I must play in that city or leave a business in which I have spent my life to attain proficiency. . . . No corporation in the world can say "You must" or "You must not" to a man except the ones conducted by the present baseball magnates.

—LARRY TWITCHELL, outfielder (1889)

A well-paid slave is nonetheless a slave.

—CURT FLOOD

The essential dignity of equals sitting down together just can't be overemphasized.

—MARVIN MILLER

Baseball owners may be the last of the great individualists. It makes many of them go crazy to talk about cooperation.

—MARVIN MILLER

The owners aren't bad. They're dumb. Marvin Miller thinks about tomorrow. They think about yesterday.

—PAUL RICHARDS

The only way to teach a magnate anything is with a club.

—Baseball Magazine (1915)

All football has to do is play its games, and the baseball owners will chase their public to them with their ignorant greed.

—JIMMY CANNON

A baseball team is a commercial venture, operating for a profit. The idea that you don't have to package your product as attractively as General Motors packages its product, and hustle your product the way General Motors hustles its product, is baseball's most pernicious enemy.

—BILL VEECK

Nobody in baseball is more aware of the fact that a ball club must sell baseball and win games. . . . But you don't sell your baseball without dressing it up in bright colored paper and red ribbons.

—BILL VEECK

If the team doesn't do well, the fans won't give a damn about Bugs Bunny. The only promotion is getting one more run than the other team.

—FRANK LANE, former baseball executive

It is not enough to say that baseball must be as good as any other business. Baseball has got to be better in its morality than any other business.

—KENESAW MOUNTAIN LANDIS (1921)

Baseball is a public trust, not merely a money-making industry.

—FORD FRICK

To be at its best the emphasis must be on the field of play—on the game, not the business. The fans must be able to believe that baseball is something more than a barnstorming tour, a traveling circus, or a TV spectacular.

—DOUGLASS WALLOP

Public confidence in baseball could be undermined if we find there is more legal news on the sports pages than in other parts of the paper.

—JUDGE JOHN W. OLIVER

173

Although salaries grow and contract clauses multiply, the business of baseball like the business of art is dream.

         —DONALD HALL

Baseball's status in the life of the nation is so pervasive that it would not strain the credulity to say the Court can take judicial notice that baseball is everybody's business. To put it mildly and with restraint, it would be unfortunate indeed if a fine sport and profession, which brings surcease from daily travail and an escape from the ordinary to most inhabitants of this land, were to suffer in the least because of undue concentration by any one or any group on commercial and profit considerations. The game is on higher ground; it behooves everyone to keep it there.

         —JUDGE IRVING BEN COOPER, *Flood* v. *Kuhn*
         (1970)

"Why is baseball, you ask? Because it is like charity—it never faileth. . . . And to the man . . . [who] wants something to kick about without meaning it and something to yell about that everybody around him will think more of him for yelling about—to that man baseball is the one great life-saver in the good old summer-time" —*Los Angeles Times* (1916).

13
IT'S A FAN'S GAME

O BASEBALL FANS are distinguished by their faith. They believe, they care—even though players and owners seem to have turned their backs on them. And this is no trivial thing. For, as Roger Angell has written, the capacity to care has almost gone out of our lives. Even if it's for a kid's game, this feeling of caring, and caring deeply, is to be savored.

The trouble with baseball is that the player who knows how to bat and field best is sitting in the bleachers.

—Anonymous

There is a man in the Government Hospital for the Insane who is perfectly sane on every subject except baseball. He knows more about baseball than any other man in America. The authorities have humored him so that he has been able to cover the walls of his large room with the intricate schedules of games played since baseball began. . . . He takes an astrological view of the game. He explains every defeat and every success on astrological principles. He has it all figured out. His sense has gone with it. He is the typical baseball crank.

—Boston *Globe* (1884)

All baseball fans are provincial. They don't want the best team to win, they want their *team to win.*

—ART HILL

I never saw a game without taking sides and never want to see one. There is the soul of the game.

—WARREN G. HARDING, former President of the United States

This blind, chauvinistic belief in one's own team, often against all reason, is foolish and marvelous. It is the muscle and magic of the game's attraction, and you cannot crush it.

—ART HILL

I love the crowd. Whenever I need something extra, I look up, and there it is. I keep saying to them, "Give it to me, give it to me."

—GEORGE BRETT

The true fan is not only violently partisan, but very noisy, and an expert at offering advice to the home team, sometimes in not very polite terms. I used to amuse myself with wondering what would happen if a group of fans of this order would turn up at a tennis match or a golf meet.

—W. R. BURNETT, sportswriter

Baseball is the working man's game. A baseball crowd is a beer-drinking crowd, not a mixed drink crowd.

—BILL VEECK

I have discovered, in twenty years of moving around a ball park, that the knowledge of the game is usually in inverse proportion to the price of the seats.

—BILL VEECK

If I was going to storm a pillbox, going to sheer utter, certain death, and the colonel said, "Shepherd, pick six guys," I'd pick six White Sox fans, because they have known death every day of their lives and it holds no terror for them.

—JEAN SHEPHERD

The crowds that watch [baseball] average about as low in sportsmanship as a mass of human beings that can be found anywhere.

—*The New York Times* (1922)

The old fans yelled, "Kill the umpire!" The new fan tries to do it.

—DR. ARNOLD BESSIER

They have Easter egg hunts in Philadelphia, and if the kids don't find the eggs, they get booed.

—BOB UECKER

Philadelphia fans would even boo a funeral.

—BO BELINSKY

Fans don't boo nobodies.

—REGGIE JACKSON

What is both surprising and delightful is that the spectators are allowed, and even expected, to join in the vocal part of the game. I do not see why this feature should not be introduced into cricket.

177

There is no reason why the field should not try to put the batsmen off his stroke at the critical moment by neatly timed disparagements of his wife's fidelity and his mother's respectability.

—GEORGE BERNARD SHAW

An ardent supporter of the hometown team should go to a game prepared to take offense, no matter what happens.

—ROBERT BENCHLEY

My wife says I am a vindictive man when it comes to baseball; I believe she is right. In the bleachers, however, you can be vindictive. Nearly everybody else is.

—ARNOLD HANO

Some day I would like to go up in the stands and boo some fans.

—BO BELINSKY

New York is a lion's den. It's the greatest place to play but also the most difficult. It can be Disneyland or it can be Hell.

—REGGIE JACKSON

I could never play in New York. The first time I ever came into a game there, I got in the bull pen car and they told me to lock the doors.

—MIKE FLANAGAN, Orioles pitcher

I'd root for the Russians over the Yankees.

—Long-time Dodger fan

All literary men are Red Sox fans. To be a Yankee fan in literary society is to endanger your life.

—JOHN CHEEVER

To Dodgers customers, their games are entertainment; to us, Red Sox games are certificates of survival, renewal and rebirth.

—GEORGE V. HIGGINS

Fenway Park, in Boston, is a lyric little bandbox of a ball park. Everything is painted green and seems in curiously sharp focus, like the inside of an old-fashioned peeping-type Easter egg.

—JOHN UPDIKE

A jai alai court with foul lines.

> —WILLIAM LEGGETT, sportswriter, on Fenway
> Park

The first big league game I ever saw was at the Polo Grounds. My father took me. I remember it so well—the green grass and the green stands. It was like seeing Oz.

> —JOHN CURTIS, pitcher

You can talk all you like about Brooklyn and New York, Minneapolis and St. Paul, Dallas and Fort Worth, but there are no two cities in America where the people want to beat each other's brains out more than in San Francisco and Los Angeles.

> —JOE CRONIN

A business executive is standing in his office looking down over the city and dictating to his secretary. Suddenly, a falling figure shoots past the window, "Oh, oh," the man says. "It must be June. There go the Giants."

> —JIM MURRAY

The man who wants to see a baseball game in the worst way should take his wife along.

> —Anonymous

One of the chief duties of the fan is to engage in arguments with the man behind him. This department of the game has been allowed to run down fearfully.

> —ROBERT BENCHLEY

First in war, first in peace, and last in the American League.

> —Proverbial remark about the Washington
> Senators

For the Washington Senators, the worst time of the year is the baseball season.

> —ROGER KAHN

It's better to be involved with a loser. A winning team doesn't need you as much.

> —BILL JAMES, baseball statistician

Flying in to Cleveland last night I thought of life in this great American city and decided that if you were going to crash on a Cleveland flight it would be better if it was an inbound flight.

—JIM BOUTON

The only good thing about playing in Cleveland is you don't have to make road trips there.

—RICHIE SCHEINBLUM, former Indian outfielder

I went through Cleveland one day, and it was closed.

—JAY JOHNSTONE, outfielder

If you look in the stands in Arlington, you see some pretty nice scenery. In Detroit all you're likely to see is a fight.

—JIMMY PIERSALL

Cincinnati is nuts with baseball! They ought to call this town Cincinnutty!

—BUGS BAER (1919)

A baseball fan has the digestive apparatus of a billy goat. He can—and does—devour any set of statistics with insatiable appetite and then nuzzle hungrily for more.

—ARTHUR DALEY, sportswriter

I don't think baseball could survive without all the statistical appurtenances involved in calculating pitching, hitting and fielding percentages. Some people could do without the games as long as they got the box scores.

—JOHN M. CULKIN

Wrigley Field is a Peter Pan of a ball park. It has never grown up and it has never grown old. Let the world race on—they'll still be playing day baseball in the friendly confines of Wrigley Field, outfielders will still leap up against the vines, and the Cubs . . . well, it's the season of hope. This could be the Cubbies' year.

—E. M. SWIFT, sportswriter

The Chicago Cub fans are the greatest fans in baseball. They've got to be.

—HERMAN FRANKS, former Cubs manager

If you can just play .500 ball for Cub fans they are happy. Can you imagine what they'd be like if you ever won a pennant for them?

—HERMAN FRANKS

All baseball fans believe in miracles, the question is, how many do you believe in?

—JOHN UPDIKE

In the deepest sediment of my soul, I know that the Cubs have been good for me. They have taught me the first rule of reasonable living: discern the inevitable and submit to it without tears.

—GEORGE F. WILL

You amaze me. The resiliency of you, the fan, amazes me. The owner drops you, moving what you thought was your team, and you bounce back. The players drop you, jumping sometimes in the middle of a cheer, but you always bounce back. . . . The owners don't give a damn. The players don't give a damn. Only you give a damn. You continue to root for a city's name on a shirt. Did you ever stop to wonder why?

—DICK YOUNG

I played the game the same every time—because I was playing for the fans, not for me. It's their game.

—WILLIE MAYS

14
BASEBALL IS FOREVER

O BASEBALL IS a triple with the bases loaded. Baseball is stealing home. Baseball is sitting in the bleachers on a sunshiny summer day, and I don't care if I never come back. Baseball is beer, peanuts and a dog. Baseball is chaw and great expectorations. Baseball is the shoe-string catch, the headfirst slide, the play at the plate. Baseball is waiting, waiting, waiting, then boom! Baseball is . . .

Baseball is more than a game with me, it's a religion.

—BILL KLEM, Hall-of-Fame umpire

Baseball is a game to be savored rather than taken in gulps.

—BILL VEECK

Baseball is a game of inches.

—BRANCH RICKEY (attributed)

Baseball is a matter of razor-edge precision. It's not a game of inches, like you hear people say. It's a game of hundredths *of inches.*

—RUBE BRESSLER

The ball once struck off,
Away flies the boy
To the next destined post,
And then home with joy.
—Anonymous (1774)

*Ninety feet between bases is the nearest to perfection that man
has yet achieved.*

—RED SMITH

*Close don't count in baseball. Close only counts in horseshoes
and hand grenades.*

—FRANK ROBINSON

Baseball is beautiful—the supreme performing art. It combines in perfect harmony the magnificent features of ballet, drama, art and ingenuity.

—BOWIE KUHN

Baseball is one of the arts.

—TED WILLIAMS

Baseball is a kind of collective chess with arms and legs in full play under sunlight.

—JACQUES BARZUN

More than other games, baseball gives its players space—both physical and emotional—in which to define themselves.

—JOHN ESKOW

I don't think you can think too hard. Baseball, when you really analyze it, is a game within a game within a game.

—SKIP LOCKWOOD

There are only five things you can do in baseball—run, throw, catch, hit and hit with power.

—LEO DUROCHER

Pitching is seventy-five percent of baseball.

—CONNIE MACK

Baseball is the only sport I know that when you're on offense, the other team controls the ball.

—KEN HARRELSON

You can't freeze the ball in this game. You have to play till the last man is out.

—JOE MCCARTHY

If horses won't eat it, I don't want to play on it.

—DICK ALLEN, on Astroturf

Keep your eye clear and hit 'em where they ain't.

—WILLIE KEELER, on the secret of hitting

"Baseball was made for kids, and grown-ups only screw it up."
—Bob Lemon

The batter is one lone man playing the other nine men.
—PAUL GALLICO

Baseball is a peculiar profession, possibly the only one which capitalizes a boyhood pleasure, unfits the athlete for any other career, keeps him young in mind and spirit, and then rejects him as too old, before he has yet attained the prime of life.
—GERALD BEAUMONT

Baseball is simply a dramatization of the life struggle of a man.
—WALTER JOHNSON

Ball teams are like human beings. They are born, live and die.
—ED BARROW

Yessuh, baseball is more than a little bit like life.

—RED BARBER

Baseball is for the leisurely afternoons of summer and for the unchanging dreams.

—ROGER KAHN

To play this game good, a lot of you has got to be a little boy.

—ROY CAMPANELLA

Baseball gives every American boy a chance to excel. Not just to be as good as someone else, but to be better. This is the nature of man and the name of the game.

—TED WILLIAMS

Baseball is the only game left for people. To play basketball, you have to be 7'6". To play football, you have to be the same width.

—BILL VEECK

They expect an umpire to be perfect on opening day and to improve as the season goes on.

—NESTOR CHYLAK, umpire

I never missed one in my heart.

—BILL KLEM

Baseball gives you every chance to be great. Then it puts every pressure on you to prove that you haven't got what it takes. It never takes away the chance, and it never eases up on the pressure.

—JOE GARAGIOLA

Let's play two!

—ERNIE BANKS

The great thing about baseball is that there's a crisis every day.

—GABE PAUL

In baseball, the expected is always happening when it's least expected, and vice versa.

—Saying

Managers don't resign. They're fired.
　　　　　　　　　—WALTER ALSTON (attributed)

Don't look back. Something might be gaining on you.
　　　　　　　　　—SATCHEL PAIGE

Catching a fly ball is a pleasure but knowing what to do with it after you catch it is a business.
　　　　　　　　　—TOMMY HENRICH, Yankee outfielder

Play ball! means something more than runs
Or pitches thudding into gloves!
Remember through the summer suns
This is the game your country loves.
—Grantland Rice

You don't play baseball, you work at baseball.
—FRED HANEY

Baseball is the only place in life where a sacrifice is appreciated.
—Saying

Baseball players, like poets, are born not made.
—MILLER HUGGINS

Ballplayers are born. If they are cut out for baseball, if they have the desire and the ambition, they will make it. That's all there is to it.
—WALTER JOHNSON

Every boy likes baseball, and if he doesn't he's not a boy.
—ZANE GREY

Nearly every boy builds a shrine to some baseball hero, and before that shrine a candle always burns.
—KENESAW MOUNTAIN LANDIS

There is nothing better calculated than baseball to give a growing boy self-poise and self-reliance.
—ALBERT SPALDING, Hall-of-Fame baseball pioneer

Give a boy a bat and a ball and a place to play and you'll have a good citizen.
—JOE MCCARTHY

For the parent of a Little Leaguer, a baseball game is simply a nervous breakdown divided into nine innings.
—EARL WILSON

Why do I like baseball? The pay is good, it keeps you out in the fresh air and sunshine, and you can't beat the hours.
—TIM HURST, umpire

Ballplayers are human, too.
—RALPH HOUK

You don't save a pitcher for tomorrow. Tomorrow it may rain.

    —LEO DUROCHER

In baseball, you don't know nothing.

    —YOGI BERRA

He ain't nothin' till I say so.

    —BILL GUTHRIE, umpire

Baseball is an island of activity amidst a sea of statistics.

    —Anonymous

You could look it up.

    —CASEY STENGEL

Be in a hurry to win. Don't be in a hurry to lose.

    —JOHN MCGRAW

Ballplayers who are first into the dining room are usually last in the averages.

    —JIMMY CANNON

I'd rather be lucky than good.

    —LEFTY GOMEZ (attributed)

Luck is the residue of design.

    —BRANCH RICKEY

Dugout to dugout, the game happily remains unchanged in our changing world.

    —BILL VEECK

They still can't steal first base.

    —PHIL RIZZUTO

Because baseball changes so little, it renews itself each year without effort, but always with feeling.

    —ROGER ANGELL

Within the ballpark, time moves differently, marked by no clock except the events of the game. . . . Since baseball time is measured only in outs, all you have to do is succeed utterly; keep hitting, keep the rally alive, and you have defeated time. You remain forever young.

—ROGER ANGELL

Some things don't need changing—the sunrise doesn't need changing, moonlight doesn't need changing, azaleas don't need changing, baseball doesn't need changing.

—TED TURNER

Baseball is almost the only orderly thing in a very unorderly world. If you get three strikes, even the best lawyer in the world can't get you off.

—BILL VEECK

The game's not over until it's over.

—YOGI BERRA

You got to get twenty-seven outs to win.

—CASEY STENGEL

Baseball is not so much an event as it is a fact of life. Sometimes we forget how much pleasure it can give.

—BILL GILES, baseball executive

Nice guys finish last.

—LEO DUROCHER

You gotta believe!

—TUG McGRAW

You can observe a lot just by watching.

—YOGI BERRA

If you're not having fun in baseball, you miss the point of everything.

—CHRIS CHAMBLISS

Baseball is very big at the present time. This makes me think baseball will live longer than Casey Stengel or anybody else.

—CASEY STENGEL

PHOTO CREDITS

14: UPI.

17–19: *San Francisco Chronicle.*

20: UPI.

27: San Francisco Giants.

29–33: National Baseball Hall of Fame.

35–44: UPI.

47–51: National Baseball Hall of Fame.

53: UPI.

56: (both) WTTW, Channel 11, Chicago Public Television.

57: National Baseball Hall of Fame.

59–64: UPI.

67: Los Angeles Dodgers.

69: National Baseball Hall of Fame.

71–80: UPI.

83: Wide World Photos.

84: Philadelphia Phillies.

85–101: UPI.

102–105: Los Angeles Dodgers.

107: *San Francisco Chronicle.*

108: UPI.

109: San Francisco Giants.

111: UPI.

112: (both) New York Mets.

115: UPI.

118: *The Sporting News.*

120: Baltimore Orioles.

122: (top) Atlanta Braves; (bottom) *San Francisco Chronicle.*

124: UPI.

127: California Angels.

128–35: UPI.

138: Philadelphia Phillies.

140: UPI.

143: California Angels.

144: Los Angeles Dodgers.

147: Kansas City Royals.

149–151: UPI.

153: Los Angeles Dodgers.
154–58: UPI.
160: Kenneth Lee.
163: Detroit Tigers.
164: (top) New York Mets; (bottom) Kansas City Royals.
165: New York Mets.
169: UPI.
171: Office of the Commissioner.
172: *San Francisco Chronicle.*
175–81: UPI.

YOU CAN LOOK IT UP

195

196

200